LEADING
WITH CAPABILITIES

LEADING
WITH CAPABILITIES

Capability-Based Management as a
Driver for Strategy Implementation

JONAS VAN RIEL

GRAMMAR
FACTORY
— EST² 2013 —

Grammar Factory Publishing
MacMillan Company Limited
25 Telegram Mews, 39th Floor, Suite 3906
Toronto, Ontario, Canada
M5V 3Z1

www.grammarfactory.com

Van Riel, Jonas.
Leading with Capabilities: Capability-Based Management as a Driver for Strategy
Implementation / Jonas Van Riel.

Paperback ISBN 978-1-998528-22-6
eBook ISBN 978-1-998528-23-3

1. BUSINESS & ECONOMICS / Strategic Planning.
2. BUSINESS & ECONOMICS / Management / General.
3. BUSINESS & ECONOMICS / Organizational Development.

Production Credits
Cover design by Designerbility
Interior layout design by Setareh Ashrafologhalai
Book production and editorial services by Grammar Factory Publishing

Grammar Factory's Carbon Neutral Publishing Commitment
Grammar Factory Publishing is proud to be neutralizing the carbon
footprint of all printed copies of its authors' books printed by or ordered
directly through Grammar Factory or its affiliated companies through
the purchase of Gold Standard-Certified International Offsets.

Disclaimer
This book is based on true events. However, in order to protect the
privacy of individuals involved, some names, locations and identifying
details have been changed or omitted. Any resemblance to persons
living or deceased, outside of the intended depictions, is purely coincidental.
The content of this book is presented with the utmost respect for all those
affected by the events described. While every effort has been made to
ensure accuracy, certain aspects of the narrative may reflect the author's
interpretation or be reconstructed from publicly available records,
personal interviews and other sources. Readers are advised that the book
contains content that may be distressing. Discretion is strongly advised.

CONTENTS

PREFACE AND ACKNOWLEDGEMENTS

F YOU'RE reading this, I assume you're interested in Capability-Based Management (CBM), a framework designed to help you achieve your strategic ambitions by addressing alignment issues and overcoming indecisiveness. That's great, because that's exactly what this book is for! My dream is that you might pick up this book in an airport bookstore, read it on your flight, and feel inspired to start applying CBM as soon as you land. But no matter where or how you come across it, I'm thrilled that you're intrigued by this novel approach to strategy implementation. As you may already sense, I'm deeply passionate about this topic, and I'd love to share why.

When I began my career as a consultant, I worked on several ERP (Enterprise Resource Planning software, like SAP) implementations. These projects entailed significant organizational transformations that involved introducing new technology, information models, and processes. A key part of these projects was conducting a Fit-Gap analysis to assess whether the ERP system aligned with the organization and what adjustments were needed for a better fit. In practice however, this was more often than not an unsolvable puzzle that led to organizations being unsure of their direction, while vendors confidently claimed they could meet every need. In my experience, the root of the problem was that organizations struggled to translate their strategic vision into clear expectations for their various operational domains. Time and again, they would dive far too deeply into operational details, losing focus and ultimately failing to properly assess the ERP software or effectively steer the implementation.

The introduction of Business Process Management (BPM) helped such organizations (and us) to better understand their processes and how ERP systems are mapped to them. However, this approach had its limitations. Firstly, in practice and far too often, the focus was on automating existing processes rather than questioning and improving them, because people were working too much on the AS-IS situation.

Second, the effort required to map these processes often led to missed timelines—as there was simply too much to map, leading people to have in-depth discussions about details rather than the bigger picture—and underutilized work. But most importantly, again, it caused senior management to get overly involved in operational questions, neglecting strategic decisions.

Later, as I delved into Enterprise Architecture, we still grappled with shaping organization-wide transformations. BPM didn't cover all aspects, and remained too operationally focused. When I first encountered the concept of a Business Capability, I was immediately impressed by its simplicity and the potential solution it offered for my earlier challenges. It allowed me to roll up operational information to a level where strategic decisions could be made. Correspondingly, it enabled senior management to communicate decisions for functional domains (capabilities), which could then be translated into operational dimensions—in other words, translate strategic decisions towards the operations.

The true value of the Capability concept, I feel, lies in this layer of abstraction and the application of systems thinking—viewing the organization as a whole comprised of interconnected parts. This holistic view allows us to analyze the entire organization *and* its individual components, but never separate from each other. The cover of this book shows a building made of Lego bricks, symbolizing an organization constructed from various building blocks over time by different people. This structure may never be perfect, but understanding its components and how they fit together is crucial for maintaining stability as the organization evolves.

Providing direction to the organization is one of senior management's most vital responsibilities, guiding employees and enabling them to excel. This book has a dual purpose: to inspire readers about the concept of CBM, and to offer an actionable tool to help organizations achieve their strategic ambitions. CBM is a relatively new idea, based on the nascent Business Capability concept. Therefore, this book isn't rooted in exact science or extensive case studies: instead, I suggest you approach it as a source of inspiration, with guidelines on starting with CBM. It combines practical experience and academic research to ensure the content is valid and relevant for managers of all levels, as well as analysts, business and IT architects, students, and fellow academics.

My hope is that you, dear reader, will adopt CBM and contribute to its growth. Use it, test it, improve it, and share your experiences far and wide. You can find contact details in the final chapter if you wish to reach out.

I want to thank several people who were invaluable in the writing of this book. Firstly, Prof. Jan Verelst, who leads the MIS program at the University of Antwerp and inspired us all in his courses on systems analysis and design, effectively introducing us to the world of systems thinking.

Next, Prof. Manu De Backer, who supervised my first master's thesis on BPM, sparking my initial interest in academics and Business Architecture.

Prof. Stijn Viaene of Vlerick, whose enthusiasm during our conversations ignited many great ideas.

Prof. Emeritus Aimé Heene of Ghent University, Prof. Monique Snoeck of KUL, and Prof. Wim Laurier of Université Saint-Louis, for so many enriching conversations while organizing an MSC in Enterprise Architecture program.

Prof. Georgios Koutsopoulos of Stockholm University— our multiple conversations on the foundational side of capabilities are always inspiring.

Finally, a special thank you to Prof. Geert Poels, my PhD supervisor, whose advice, along with his extraordinary patience and critical mind, has been invaluable throughout my challenging journey of balancing a PhD with full-time consultancy and teaching. To the many great colleagues and customers who helped shape my ideas over the years, I extend my heartfelt gratitude.

Finally, a profound thank you to my wonderful wife, who never ceases to motivate me in her own kind way. And to my parents, who made it possible for me to pursue my dreams.

CHAPTER 1

BRINGING YOUR STRATEGIC VISION TO LIFE
Strategy Implementation and Organizational Transformation

"Strategy execution is as important, if not more important, as strategy formulation."

JAMES M. HIGGINS

VERY ORGANIZATION should have a vision of its future—a version of itself that's more effective, innovative, or profitable. However, realizing this future state is far from straightforward, particularly in today's volatile, uncertain, complex, and ambiguous (VUCA) world [1]. Rapid technological advances and economic fluctuations pose daunting challenges, pushing organizations to undertake transformative journeys often filled with complexities.

Take digital transformation, which is the cornerstone of many such journeys—and a monumental task. It goes beyond mere incorporation of digital technologies: it's about reinventing business models with new digital offerings and overhauling operational processes to enhance efficiency, at the same time keeping an eye on their environmental impact [2]. However, the path to successful digital transformation is often fraught with obstacles. Stijn Viaene, a professor at the Vlerick Business School in Belgium, underlines a crucial point when he notes that one of the key reasons organizations struggle with digital transformation is the lack of a shared perspective and a common language [3]. Other scientific research echoes this sentiment [4], stressing that coherence—or the lack thereof—can significantly impact an organization's ability to create business value amid digital disruptions.

Whether we're talking about a tech-focused challenge or not, it's no secret that organizations often find it tough to bring their strategic visions to life. This struggle usually boils down to the absence of two crucial things: coherence, and a shared understanding or perspective, the lack of which causes alignment issues. Enterprise Architecture (EA) holds the key to tackle these issues. But how?

The three hats of Enterprise Architecture

EA is a discipline that has been highlighted in research by scholars like Jeanne W. Ross at MIT [5] and others [6, 7]. Their work circles around a core theme—*clearer insights and better communication lead to improved alignment and, ultimately, smarter decisions.*

So, whether you're in the throes of a digital transformation or simply trying to execute a strategic vision, remember this key message: *Improved insights and communication aren't just nice to have—they're essential for making better decisions and driving your organization forward.*

For those unfamiliar with the concept, Enterprise Architecture, a practice central to many organizations, wears three hats: it is a *value creator*, a *coherence maker*, and a *strategy aligner*. Now, what do these terms mean in practice?

As a **value creator**, EA looks at all the parts that make up an enterprise—the roles people have, the processes they follow, the information they use, the applications they interact with, and the technology they employ—and ensures that these are all working towards the organization's goal: to create value.

When we talk about EA as a **coherence maker**, we're saying that all these different parts of the enterprise shouldn't just be doing their own thing: rather, they should be working together to form a cohesive whole, like gears in a machine. They're not just aligned, they're *integrated*, functioning as a coherent system where all the pieces support each other. The idea here is that we don't want to achieve local optimization, we want to optimize the whole.

The hat of a **strategy aligner** takes the previous two topics one step further. Coherence and value creation are great steps, but they need to be put in the direction envisioned by the owners or senior management team. Simply put, different parts of an organization can create a sort of scattered and sub-optimal value, without really working together. And, even if they're working together, they might not be focused on strategic ambitions and vision.

Imagine a well-oiled organization focusing on outdated services or products but ignoring the vision of its management, which is aimed at keeping up with the changes in the market. So, combining these three hats implies that EA takes the big picture—those strategic decisions about how the organization will create value—and translates it into a detailed plan for the organization to execute.

This plan, often referred to as the "Enterprise Architecture blueprint and roadmap," shows how every resource is directed towards the common goal of value creation. It's like a map that guides the organization towards achieving its strategic objectives and overall vision. This immediately illustrates the value of EA as the primary challenger of strategic vision. If the vision is unclear, it's impossible to wear all three hats and create a proper plan for implementation.

Creating a model of the future enterprise

The creation of this map is driven by a practice known as *enterprise modeling.*

Enterprise modeling involves designing models of what the future of the enterprise might look like. Far more than just a technical exercise, it's a strategic tool for envisioning and planning the next steps, enabling organizations to adapt and grow effectively. Although it sounds somewhat technical, Enterprise Architecture plays a crucial role in an organization's strategy by creating value, maintaining coherence, and aligning with the broader vision. In doing so, it addresses the need for a shared understanding—something that many organizations struggle with.

The critique that Enterprise Architecture focuses too much on these models is, in reality, a critique of those who misuse the practice. The models themselves are never the ultimate goal: rather, they are invaluable tools that help us understand the context, foster mutual understanding, and chart a course for where we need to go. It's akin to what Gerard Mercator (Antwerp-born, like me) did when he created maps of the world in the 16th century. His maps were not an end in themselves—their true value lay in helping his customers navigate the world.

There are multiple modeling techniques and methods that can be applied when practicing EA, such as value streams, landscape models, and technology models. I believe, however, that EA can take two perspectives. First, a more managerial perspective, where we focus on bringing guidance and overview at a higher level. Second, a perspective I call "completeness and correctness," where the focus lies on making sure the organization as a system works well on different levels.

However, I am firmly convinced that the initial step in an Enterprise Architecture practice should be to prioritize the first perspective of higher-level alignment and guidance. By abstracting from the operational details and information, this approach enables us to first concentrate on the foundational questions related to the more structural topics. A low-threshold concept that can bring value quite easily, and allows us to focus initially on that first perspective, is that of capabilities.

Capabilities—our gateway to decision-making

Capabilities offer a gateway to creating a meaningful blueprint for the organization. It provides us with a layer in between the strategic and operational level, which we can then use to base important (management) decisions on.

For this reason, this book introduces the practice of Capability-Based Management (CBM). Through experience as a consultant and research, I have learned that the Capability concept offers us a helping hand in multiple scenarios (I will explain more about this later).

But first things first. In the next chapter, we will delve into the concepts of capabilities, capability structures, and the visual models called Capability Maps (or CapMaps), which are crucial concepts in the practice of Enterprise Architecture.

The CapMap essentially serves as a graphical canvas—a vista filled with information upon which you make your informed decisions. It may sound abstract right now, but trust me, it will all become clearer as we dive deeper and learn how to construct these maps, which will serve as our compasses in navigating the challenges ahead. This book is your practical guide if you're keen on exploring CBM and ultimately improving your ability to implement a strategic vision.

CapMaps—our touchstone for decision-making

Creating a CapMap is one thing, but how exactly do we use it? In this book, I refer to the various applications of the Cap-Map as its "Use Cases," which are the central pillars of CBM.

The term "CBM" was chosen intentionally to underscore that a CapMap is our touchstone for making management decisions. CBM's goal is very straightforward: it's intended to help you manage your organization more effectively and bring your ambitions to fruition by providing a tool that answers the call for increased coherence, and a shared understanding or perspective within the organization.

Once we've tackled the primary Use Cases of a CapMap, we'll navigate through specific scenarios that showcase how these Use Cases can come in handy in certain situations, from a digital transformation to other types of challenges. These scenarios will illustrate how you can utilize various CapMap Use Cases to address key questions that arise in these situations. The next two chapters provide some reflections on the different possibilities of CBM. The final chapter will then offer an overview of all Use Cases and functions.

So, strap in, and get ready for a practical journey into Capability-Based Management!

Kicking off with our guiding example
of the Royal BelFoot Football Club

When navigating capability mapping, it's immensely helpful to have a tangible reference—a realistic scenario that breathes life into the concepts we discuss. To this end, I've integrated an example that will weave its way through the chapters that follow.

Welcome to Royal BelFoot, a football club that was created around our research into capability mapping for professional sports clubs [8]. While the club itself is fictional, its challenges, dilemmas, and decisions mirror those which many organizations face.

Why choose a football club, you might ask? The choice wasn't arbitrary: my ongoing research in capability mapping has partially revolved around professional sports clubs, and I wanted to bring the insights of that research into this book. Moreover, football clubs, despite their unique product (the magic of the game), are multifaceted entities with challenges often paralleling those of conventional businesses. Strip away the game-day glamor, and you'll find that a football club functions much like any other dynamic business organization, facing all the VUCA world challenges.

So, as we journey through capability mapping, Royal BelFoot will be our guide—giving abstract concepts a realistic form, and making the principles we delve into immediately relatable and applicable.

CHAPTER 2

CAPABILITIES AND CAPMAPS
A Layer to Connect the Strategic and Operational Levels

"To learn the truth, we must put all the parts together."
"THE BLIND MEN AND THE ELEPHANT"
(AN INDIAN FOLK TALE)

AT THE UNIVERSITY, our research focuses on the practice of Capability-Based Management as an Enterprise Architecture approach to drive the strategic alignment, enterprise coherence, and value creation that organizations aspire to achieve. All of these are goals I also aim to achieve with my customers in practice. But before delving any deeper, let's define "capability."

One note, though, before we really get started: in practice, the term "capabilities" is used to refer to many things. In this book, we will focus on what is commonly referred to as a "business capability." However, as the word "business" might be seen to (unintentionally) exclude non-profit organizations, this has prompted me to argue that "Enterprise Capabilities," or "Organizational Capabilities," might be more inclusive alternatives. Since this book positions the Capability concept within the discipline of Enterprise Architecture (and CBM aligns closely with this field), the term "Enterprise Capabilities" feels like the most fitting choice and is my preference. However, to keep things simple, throughout the book I'll just use the term "capability."

Strategic management offers various theories on obtaining and sustaining a competitive advantage. Some focus on securing unique resources, others on how value is created. As Harris and Lennox from UVA Darden have explicated, the strategist's challenge lies in finding the sweet spot between an organization's capabilities (what we can do), its core values (what we stand for), and the opportunities presented by the market [9]. This nuanced interplay highlights the multifaceted nature of strategic positioning and clarifies the role of the Capability concept. In essence, a capability represents the capacity of an enterprise to attain a specific goal within a given context, necessitating the right configuration of resources and the ability to access them. Put simply, a capability underscores the "what"—as in, what should the organization be capable of doing, and how should we configure resources to realize this?

In 1996, Hamel and Prahalad [10] stated that an organization that wishes to be and stay competitive needs to answer three key questions. The first two focus on the Business Model, while the third emphasizes the importance of capabilities, and will feature heavily in this book. We will focus not only on finding these crucial capabilities, but also on deciding how they should be organized and how to develop them.

These three key questions are:

1   Which customers does your company serve today—and which will it serve in the future?

2   Who are your competitors today—and who will they be in the future?

3   Which capabilities make your firm unique today—and which will make it unique in the future?

2.1   What are (Enterprise) Capabilities?

WHAT is an organization to do?

At a high level, capabilities can be viewed as the principal operational or managerial domains within an organization. Examples of high-level domains (capabilities) include Sales, Procurement, Logistics, Financial Accounting, and so on. We call these **Level 1** capabilities. Let's take a look at logistics, for example. This high-level (Level 1) capability can be broken down into more specific capabilities, such as inbound logistics, outbound logistics, picking, packing, and so on. Each of these represents a distinct ability of the organization, and requires different resources to be effectively executed. We call these **Level 2** capabilities.

In theory, there is no limit to the number of levels. As a guiding principle, however, I recommend not going below **Level 3** capabilities unless you really feel it's required, as the scope would become too limited for strategic analysis. After all, we are aiming for a tool that helps us configure and steer the organization based on its building blocks, initially avoiding looking at the details so we can facilitate the strategic conversation. Deep diving into too granular a structure would open the door to too operational a conversation, and it would also become more difficult to link other concepts, such as processes, as they would span too many capabilities.

I've provided an example below to make all of this a little more tangible:

This scenario offers two examples of capabilities. The first is a Level 1 capability with 3 child capabilities. The second is a Level 2 capability— an example of one of the 3 child capabilities, and a further (partial) decomposition of the first.

EXAMPLE 1

Capability: Marketing and Sales Management (Level 1)

Description: At Royal BelFoot Football Club, the Sales and Marketing capability is central to nurturing the club's relationship with its fans, while simultaneously capitalizing on its commercial opportunities. It blends marketing efforts for fan engagement, Brand Strategy to carve a compelling club narrative, and Sales Management to drive revenue from ticket sales, merchandise, and sponsorships. Together, these help ensure that Royal BelFoot shines on and off the field, resonating with fans and ensuring commercial success.

Child capabilities: Marketing, Brand Strategy Implementation, Sales Management

EXAMPLE 2

Capability: Marketing (Level 2; parent capability is Marketing and Sales Management)

Description: At Royal BelFoot Football Club, the Marketing capability plays a crucial role in forging fan and corporate relationships. This encompasses the strategic planning for promoting merchandise, ticketing options for fans, and exclusive B2B opportunities, including sponsorships and premium hospitality. By blending these elements, the club ensures a consistent and compelling message across its consumer and business-facing fronts.

Child Capabilities: Marketing Strategy Development; Marketing of Merchandise; Marketing of B2C ticket options; Marketing of B2B sponsorship programs; Marketing of B2B hospitality and arrangements; Marketing of game-day products and services; Marketing of B2B ticket options

HOW is an organization to do it?

Understanding *what* a business needs to do (the capability) is only part of the equation. To fully realize this capability, we also need to establish *how* to do it. This "how" revolves around the specific configuration of different dimensions that represent the various resources an organization must acquire and manage effectively, encompassing processes, information, people, other resources, and technology. Combining these dimensions into an effective system that works is as important as having a clear and focused goal.

Given that Enterprise Capabilities are first and foremost an organizational-oriented concept, it's interesting to look into the concept of a Work System. As defined by Prof. Steven Alter, a Work System is "a system in which human participants and/or machines perform processes and activities using information, technology, and other resources to produce specific product/services for specific internal or external customers" [11]. This fits what we're trying to achieve when translating the strategic ambitions into a system or model for execution, depending on the specific configuration of the resources. Today, the term "operating model" is more widely used than "Work System," but this is, in essence, quite similar—although it doesn't put emphasis as much on business first. The operating model of an organization is the combination of the operating models of its capabilities. In other words, a capability first states the WHAT, but organizing and implementing the WHAT requires the organization to operationalize their vision of the different capabilities through their operating models, requiring the organization to configure the operational resources of each individual capability (HOW).

Multiple takes on the different (operating-model) dimensions of a capability exist, but I prefer to focus on five dimensions which each reflect the resources and structures that we need:

- **Processes** refers to the series of actions or operations conducted to achieve a particular outcome.

- **Information** represents the valuable data that informs these processes.

- **People** are the individuals with the necessary competencies and expertise to carry out these processes. This dimension includes how to organize people, which is where team structures and collaboration models come into play. I also like to include the concept of *culture* here, as I believe culture plays an important role in realizing the type of capability you want to organize. (More on that later.)

- **Other resources** can include tangible and non-tangible resources, such as physical assets (e.g., tools, machines), intellectual capital (e.g., patents, IP), or anything else the organization needs to function.

- **Technology** refers to the digital tools and systems that support and optimize these processes.

A view on the value of using capabilities

Capabilities are closely related to the Resource-Based View (RBV) of the firm theory [12, 13, 14], a strategic management framework that emphasizes the importance of a company's internal resources as the primary drivers of competitive advantage and superior performance. According to the RBV, firms are seen as unique bundles of resources and capabilities, and it is the effective management and deployment of these that determine success in the marketplace. Resources, in this context, include tangible assets such as capital, equipment, and facilities, as well as intangible assets like brand reputation, intellectual property, and organizational knowledge. However, simply having valuable resources isn't enough—

the true strength of a firm lies in its capabilities, which enable it to utilize its resources effectively in order to achieve desired outcomes.

Capabilities essentially represent what the organization needs to do (i.e., what capabilities it should have) and how these should be operationalized (i.e., how the resources need to be configured) to transform them into valuable products and services. By focusing on developing and enhancing these capabilities, firms can create a sustainable competitive advantage difficult for competitors to replicate—a sentiment expressed by David J. Teece [15], who states that the long-term success of a firm hinges not only on accumulating resources and strategic positioning, but also on continuous learning, regular refinement, and the effective management of intangible assets and other resources. To ensure the enterprise's health, that resource management needs to be viewed as equally important as resource acquisition.

Teece and his co-authors further introduced the concept of "dynamic capabilities" in 1997 [16], defining them as "the firm's ability to integrate, build, and reconfigure internal and external competences to address rapidly changing environments. Dynamic capabilities thus reflect an organization's ability to achieve new and innovative forms of competitive advantage given path dependencies and market positions." Later in this book, we'll delve into the evolution of capabilities and the difference between more standardized, market-conforming capabilities and innovative capabilities. Naturally, the outside-in look (such as analyzing competitors and customers) shouldn't be forgotten, since it's important to decide which capabilities are needed and how they should be organized.

By aligning capabilities with strategic objectives, organizations can ensure that their resources are effectively leveraged, driving long-term success and resilience in a

competitive landscape. By dynamically configuring operational dimensions, an organization shapes its capabilities.
It's through this holistic approach—addressing both *what*
we need to do and *how* to do it—that an organization can
fulfill its strategic ambitions. In a nutshell, capabilities are
not just about the *what*, but also about managing and aligning the configurations of resources—the *how*—so that we
can execute the *what* effectively and efficiently. Here lies the
first real value of the Capability concept: we break the organization down into smaller domains, allowing us to solve
the puzzle in a more feasible way. The crux, however, is to
remember that that these domains are not standalone building blocks, but rather will be related or connected through
processes and applications. Remember, we're looking at the
organization as an interwoven system of components.

We will cover how precisely to use the decisions made at
capability level to design the operating model later, but the
general idea here is that by making decisions at the capability level based on strategic ambitions and vision, we imply
guidelines that can then be used to make the right decisions
on the operating model dimension. An important part of
bringing purpose and focus to the actual operating model
through the concept of capabilities are the key performance
indicators (KPIs) that can be defined at the capability level.
These allow us to measure and express how well we are
doing compared to targets, and determine whether the
mix of resources we're putting together is actually working.
(Again, more on that later.)

Now, how does the concept of capability differ from a
process or process groups? The difference is that while both
are integral to an organization's operations, capabilities offer
a more abstract definition of the organization's scope, thus
reducing complexity for the initial analysis on a strategic

level. This is the second true value of applying the Capability concept. Defining the boundaries of processes can be challenging, especially when attempting to avoid overlap and subdividing larger processes into smaller ones. This intricate delineation often results in the entanglement of sub-processes, further increasing the complexity. We circumvent this by initially abstracting the "how" in capability definition. While it's crucial to eventually connect the "what" to the "how," this linkage can be made at a later stage, and can often safely remain abstract when represented in a CapMap. (We'll look into this more later in the book.)

A third advantage of the Capability concept is that it allows us to encompass more than just processes. Capabilities involve a mix of resources and processes (such as IT applications), while processes are just one element. Even more interesting, multiple processes can realize a single capability and vice versa. The same applies to IT applications, which can support multiple capabilities. I don't consider this a limitation, as it allows us to shield specific viewpoints and conversations from the complexity of the resource mix in an organization. Furthermore, when linking a specific process to multiple capabilities, this already offers a new insight as it implies an additional level of complexity, where different domains are dependent on each other or even collaborate. The same is true when multiple capabilities are realized by a single IT application.

In short, the abstraction and stability that capabilities provide make them a valuable tool for depicting organizational structure. Changes often occur in the "how" but less so in the "what," making for a more coherent view of the organization and facilitating alignment. This idea also aligns with the time horizon related to strategic decision-making. In general, strategic decisions are kept stable for a longer period, around three years. This means that we don't need to revalidate these decisions several times a year: if there's no clear need to change them, the decisions should stand for a longer period. After all, decisions at the strategic level might have huge implications for the operating model, and often require a lot of time and money to realize. In the realm of strategic decision-making, focusing on capabilities allows for a higher-level view that helps keep sight of the overall organizational objectives, rather than getting entangled in the specifics of certain processes or IT applications. It provides the organization with guidelines that can be used to design an operating model that aligns with the strategic vision.

For instance, when considering outsourcing, it makes more sense to focus on capabilities rather than departments. The department is a configuration choice that relates to the operating model, and thus should also be considered, but the capability should come first. After all, it's "what" you do that needs to be outsourced. Moreover, capabilities outshine organization charts in depicting the functional aspects of an organization, as the latter often reflect people and political dynamics.

Lastly, let's consider costs. One could argue that cost centers or activity-based costing align well with the capability structure. If we aim to assign costs to a specific function, why not use the capability structure to collect all costs related to process execution, people, other resources, and information technology? But that's a story for another time.

2.2   What exactly are CapMaps?

A CapMap offers a structured insight into an organization's capabilities. They have been described in multiple studies [17, 18], and found their way into practice. Within such a map, the capabilities can have various statuses—planned, desired, or implemented to different extents. The dominant mode of presenting them is via a graphical map. But CapMaps are based on an underlying capability structure, defining and representing a sort of structural decomposition of your organization, showing different functional areas or domains of control. Note that a capability structure does not have to be presented as a CapMap, but can also be articulated in a textual format—referred to as a "capability catalog" or "library." (Note that before creating a CapMap, you should always create the capability structure first; more on this in Chapter 3.)

Hierarchically, capabilities can be broken down from parent to child entities, as illustrated earlier. It's also relevant to mention the interoperability of CapMaps with broader Enterprise Architecture concepts. A case in point is the Archimate language, where capability objects find associations with elements like value streams. While this is relevant and useful, this would also take us beyond the scope of this book; here, we're going to aim to provide you with a low-threshold toolset to build and use CapMaps in your organization and improve the execution of your strategic vision.

The design of a capability model is intrinsically tied to its purpose. When the intent is to link capabilities with expansive data sets, encompassing systems, evaluation metrics, or locations, a list or matrix design might be preferable rather than a CapMap. In contrast, brevity and clarity take precedence for audiences like senior management, which will likely lead you towards a more graphic CapMap. Even within this format, the amount of detail shown can vary: we can choose to highlight detailed, specific capabilities, or focus on a bigger, more general high-level view. (More on this in the next chapter.)

CapMaps—enabling enrichment and bringing value

In essence, a CapMap is a high-caliber communication instrument. Its core objective is to enable enriched conversations with stakeholders around scope, impacts, and the ramifications of decisions, projects, or applications, ultimately aiming to increase that coherence and shared understanding mentioned earlier. Perfection, while admirable, isn't the goal—effective communication and stakeholder buy-in are. Recognized as a dynamic model, it invites optimization and updates in an iterative manner, while also chasing long-term stability.

Briefly revisiting a central idea: the CapMap zeroes in on the "what," side-stepping the intricacies of the "how." It crystallizes the organization's present endeavors and future imperatives, steering clear of operational-model nuances. Notably, the resilience of a CapMap shines through in its stability. Organizational shifts might be temporary, but well-chiseled business capabilities endure, resisting change unless the business model itself undergoes a significant shift. After all, the "what" we do stays more or less the same unless we truly expand or change the business. The "how" is something that shifts and redefines itself more easily as processes evolve, technology changes, roles are reinvented, and so on.

While it's essential to construct CapMaps that don't overemphasize the motivations or structures stemming from specific departments or politics, this doesn't mean there can be no value in zooming in on a particular part of the organization. When there's a need to concentrate on a specific department, for example, creating a detailed CapMap for that department or area can be highly valuable. However, when designing a CapMap for the whole organization, it's crucial to step back from localized perspectives and biases:

instead, the focus should be on painting a comprehensive picture that truly represents the organization's holistic capabilities, free from the boundaries or biases of specific departments or individuals.

Lastly, it's important to highlight that capability mapping is not rigid. There is no single, perfect way to do it—the details of the map depend on its purpose and who it's meant for. The key concept should always be "fit-for-purpose." While there are some basic principles that almost always apply, the specifics can vary.

In the next chapter, we'll go through the key steps of making a CapMap to start building your own. But remember, the way you design your map should reflect its main purpose and the grand goals you're aiming for.

CHAPTER 3

BUILDING A CAPMAP

Structuring Your Organization's Path to Transformation

"All models are wrong, but some are useful."

GEORGE E. P. BOX

A COMMON CRITIQUE I've heard about CapMaps is that they seem overly simplistic, almost too straightforward to have any significant value. This sentiment stems from the perception that they are uncomplicated representations of an organization. And, in a way, I agree.

But the true value of a CapMap goes far deeper than this. It's not just about the map itself, but the journey and the consensus-building process that leads to its creation. When stakeholders agree that the map accurately reflects their organization, it signifies a shared understanding of the organizational landscape. This shared understanding eliminates assumptions about their business domains, ensuring everyone is speaking the same language. From this point, the map becomes a robust foundation for detailed analysis and strategic discussions (which we'll explore in Chapter 4). When people express this and acknowledge that the map represents their organizational domains, it's a win-win. It shows that the map mirrors their organizational reality and, crucially, that there's collective agreement on what this reality entails. It's always astonishing to find that, even at the highest organizational levels, assumptions are made about foundational aspects of the organization that lead to misalignment and poor decisions. Making the organization's landscape (and the related decisions) tangible and explicit is vital for clarity and alignment—and enterprise models like CapMaps are perfect tools to achieve this.

We are now going to delve into the fundamental steps for crafting a CapMap, drawing on a wealth of experience for a recommended approach. Remember that creating enterprise models isn't a rigid science: the path you take might deviate from these steps, yet still lead to an equally effective outcome. And that's perfectly okay—there's room for adaptability based on your unique context.

Following on from this, we'll explore some guiding principles that were created to act as a checklist during the mapping process, aiming to ensure comprehensiveness and clarity. We then shift focus to the use of reference models. I strongly advocate for building upon established knowledge and work, but it's crucial to use these models as guides rather than absolute truths. Lastly, we will conclude by reflecting on the various perspectives that different views of the map can offer, and why it's important to tailor these to specific objectives and needs.

3.1   Guiding principles

As already discussed, the approach to developing a CapMap can vary. However, both research [8] and practical experience have identified several guiding principles to consider when developing such a map. These include:

GUIDING PRINCIPLE 1: Iterative approach. Creating a perfectly accurate model on the first attempt is unlikely. It's essential to engage with different stakeholders, learning and refining the model as we progress. Iterations are crucial for developing a model that is representative and widely accepted.

GUIDING PRINCIPLE 2: Level 1 size limitation. Determining an appropriate level of abstraction for the highest-level capabilities is key to your CapMap being understood. Drawing from real-world experience in developing CapMaps, I recommend capping the first level at around 10 (plus or minus three) capabilities. This ensures a clear and manageable structure, particularly when presenting to senior management.

GUIDING PRINCIPLE 3: Clear and recognizable business terms. Use nouns to effectively describe a capability—solutions and technology terms are less suitable. The aim is for a label that best conveys the "what." Nouns often pair with verbs (Financial Management, for example), but if the verb is omitted, management of that domain is implied. Select terms that reflect the organization's reality and resonate with stakeholders.

GUIDING PRINCIPLE 4: Stable naming of capabilities. The "what" of an organization typically remains stable over time (barring major shifts in the business model), so avoid terms that are transient or trendy.

GUIDING PRINCIPLE 5: Mutually Exclusive and Collectively Exhaustive (MECE). Capabilities should cover all aspects of the organization (or a specific focus area like a department) without overlap between them. Such clarity prevents confusion in decision-making and responsibilities.

GUIDING PRINCIPLE 6: It's not generally recommended to start from scratch. Leverage existing industry reference models as a solid foundation, sticking to the "standing on the shoulders of giants" principle. Internal sources such as cost center or organizational structures can also offer valuable insights, though they shouldn't be adopted verbatim. (See Step A2 in the next section for more information on this.)

GUIDING PRINCIPLE 7: Content first, graphical models later. While various graphical representations are possible, an initial focus on defining the capabilities, their labels, and their scope is more efficient. This allows for the creation of multiple models based on the same core structure without unnecessary reworking. So, build a capability structure first and create the visual CapMap later.

GUIDING PRINCIPLE 8: Create descriptions for each capability. A description for each capability at every level is crucial. These descriptions foster a shared understanding of the capability's scope, which is vital for alignment. While a given term might seem simple to understand, it's common for people to interpret the same terms in different ways; explicit descriptions can help prevent such misunderstandings.

GUIDING PRINCIPLE 9: Get executive support. In general, the capability structure and corresponding CapMap are tools to facilitate strategic decisions and improve the translation of those decisions to the operational level. In practice, the adoption of the capability structure and CapMap(s) by all levels is crucial to truly activate their value. But given that the first thing to do is to make those strategic decisions, the executive level is the starting point: their buy-in is important to give the tool the right credibility.

Let's revisit the two capability examples previously discussed.

EXAMPLE 1

Capability: Marketing and Sales Management (L1). Notice that the label here is broad, implying a larger scope. This is appropriate for a Level 1 capability, where a wider scope is expected to encapsulate a significant operational domain.

Description: At Royal BelFoot Football Club, the Marketing and Sales capability is central to nurturing the club's relationship with its fans, while simultaneously capitalizing on its commercial opportunities. This capability blends Marketing efforts for fan engagement; Brand Strategy to carve a compelling club narrative; and Sales Management to drive revenue from ticket sales, merchandise, and sponsorships. Together, these facets ensure Royal BelFoot shines both on and off the field, resonating with fans and ensuring commercial success.

The description is sufficiently detailed to establish the scope. Level 1 capabilities require broad descriptions to provide clarity on their overarching scope. It's also crucial to ensure alignment between this description and those of its child capabilities.

Child capabilities: Marketing; Brand Strategy; Sales Management

EXAMPLE 2

Capability: Marketing (L2). Here, the term "Marketing" is used without the verb "Management" for the sake of clarity, assuming "management of" is implied. The focus here is on readability and familiar terminology.

Description: At Royal BelFoot Football Club, the Marketing capability plays a crucial role in forging fan and corporate relationships. This encompasses the strategic planning for promoting merchandise, ticketing options for fans, and exclusive B2B opportunities, including sponsorships and premium hospitality arrangements. By blending these elements, the club ensures a consistent and compelling messaging across its consumer and business-facing fronts.

Child capabilities: Marketing Strategy Development; Marketing of Merchandise; Marketing of B2C ticket options; Marketing of B2B sponsorship programs; Marketing of B2B hospitality and arrangements; Marketing of game-day products and services; Marketing of B2B ticket options

Now that we've explored these guiding principles, let's examine the steps for creating a CapMap that adheres to these principles.

3.2   The steps

As mentioned above, the steps to create a CapMap are not a guaranteed route to success, and should be adapted creatively to suit different situations. However, the method outlined here is grounded in research and practical experience, offering a comprehensive approach that incorporates our guiding principles and proven strategies.

The key to this approach is to work in phases and iterate within them. Observing this process across many organizations, I've often seen a rush to finalize the structure and then engage stakeholders, which is not the most effective method. It's far better to proceed through designated phases, ensuring alignment at each level before progressing to the next. In this approach, the process is divided into three main phases, and the validation step at the end of each should be seen as a gate to pass through.

PHASE A: Derive and align on Level 1
- STEP A1. Deciding on initial scope, focus, and purpose
- STEP A2. Collection of information and data
- STEP A3. Deriving and defining Level 1 + validation

PHASE B: Elaborate on the model—add Levels 2 and 3
- STEP B1. Deriving and defining Levels 2 and 3 + validation

PHASE C: Create a CapMap
- STEP C1. Decide on the scope, purpose, and target audience for the visual model (CapMap)
- STEP C2. Create and validate the visual model
- STEP C3. Distribute the model

The steps in detail

STEP A1: Deciding on initial scope, focus, and purpose. This step might seem trivial, but is quite crucial. At the start of your endeavor, consider the intended purpose and scope of the final CapMap—for example, mapping the logistics domain in Germany versus creating a global group map. Based on your objectives and available resources, define a realistic scope and identify the relevant stakeholders required for the co-creation of the capability structure to base the CapMap on. Parameters like geographical scope, organizational level (group, subsidiary, division, etc.), time-frame, and budget are all relevant. However, some caution is advised: if time and budget allows, it might be beneficial to build a capability structure that reflects the entire organization. (More on this in Step C1.)

STEP A2: Collection of information and data. This key step in developing a CapMap involves making several crucial decisions. Firstly, you should decide whether to create and distribute the map through a top-down approach involving senior management; a bottom-up approach with subject-matter experts from various domains; or a mix of both. I believe that a combined approach typically yields the most comprehensive results, ensuring commitment from the operational and strategic levels of your organization. However, if time constraints are a factor and you need to choose one over the other, the top-down method is generally quicker and easier to roll out, as it comes from senior management with their support and a clear mandate.

The next decision concerns your starting point, and is closely related to Guiding Principle 6 above—i.e., whether to build the structure from scratch (known as a "greenfield' creation), or to "adopt and adapt" by using a pre-existing template or reference model. This latter approach can kick-start the process, using models such as generic industry capability or process models (or even industry-leader best practices) as a basis. Despite different operational implementations (or operating models), organizations within the same industry or sector generally aim for similar goals and so require comparable capabilities, especially on the "what" level. A high-level, sector-specific CapMap can be adapted to the unique aspects and strategic choices of individual organizations. The same principle applies to domain reference models which cover specific domains, such as IT Management or Information Security, yet remain agnostic when it comes to industry or business context. However, remember that all these models, while valuable, may not always be publicly available or directly applicable due to confidentiality or intellectual property concerns.

When seeking reference models, I would advise exploring various sources, like industry or domain-focused organizations or academic research. For instance, our study [8] resulted in the Reference Framework for Sport Clubs (REFFS), which offered a CapMap tailored for professional sport clubs (used as an illustrative example later). Alternatively, structures and models are available for purchase. The American Productivity & Quality Center (APQC) provides excellent free material (in addition to their premium content) whose process structures can potentially inspire the development of your capability structure's first and second levels.

Regardless of the approach you choose, it's beneficial to include other organizational information when creating the capability structure. This includes reviewing the organizational structure, financial frameworks, business models, and current strategic, business, and financial plans, as well as the application landscape. These sources offer valuable insights into the organization's operational needs, and can provide information on which capabilities exist, and which are to be acquired or created, in order to realize strategic ambitions.

STEP A3: Deriving and defining Level 1 + validation. Armed with the information obtained from reference models and additional organizational insights, we can now draft the initial version of our Level 1 capability structure (not the visual CapMap yet). The approach is straightforward: develop a preliminary model, and then engage in thorough discussions with various stakeholders. It's essential to select labels and names for the capabilities that genuinely represent the organizational reality. As highlighted in Guiding Principle 2, best practice is to aim for around 10 (give or take three) capabilities at this first level in the interests clarity and manageability.

EXAMPLE CASE: REFFS CAPABILITY STRUCTURE

The Level 1 capabilities of the REFFS framework

1.0 Club Strategy Management

2.0 Products and Services Development and Management

3.0 Marketing and Sales Management

4.0 Product Delivery and Material Management

5.0 Game-day Match/Event Delivery

6.0 Customer/Fan Services and Relationship Management

7.0 Staff, Player, and Team Development/Management, Human Capital Management

8.0 Information Technology (IT) Management

9.0 Financial Resources Management/Finance and Controlling

10.0 Asset/Infrastructure Acquisition, Construction, and Management

11.0 Enterprise Risk, Compliance, Remediation, and Resiliency Management

12.0 External Relationships Management

Let's take BelFoot as an example, where the organization is using a reference framework (REFFS) as the foundation for its own CapMap. Now, let's examine how to effectively utilize a reference model during this phase of capability structuring. At this highest level, capabilities naturally encompass a broad scope, serving as the umbrella for various Level 2 and

Level 3 child capabilities. My advice is to adhere closely to a standard Level 1 framework, as most organizations share comparable high-level structures. Deviating significantly from this generic structure is generally unwarranted.

Consider a professional sports organization—in this case, BelFoot—adopting this model. They would first evaluate the relevance of each Level 1 capability. Given their overarching nature, it would be unusual for any to be deemed irrelevant. The next step involves ensuring that the names or labels accurately represent the organization's operational reality— for instance, "Game-day Match/Event Delivery" could be more aptly titled "Game-day Organization" to better reflect the context. When utilizing a standard reference structure, this step can be efficiently concise. However, if you are crafting a capability structure from the ground up, expect to invest more time. Regardless of the starting point, most of the effort will be channeled into refining and aligning the Level 2 and Level 3 capabilities, which is where the more detailed work truly lies.

It's important to recognize that the first-level capabilities may vary if the reference model employed uses a distinct logic for defining the top tier. In this example, we observe three general types of capabilities at the highest level. The first type is associated with the strategic domain of the organization, covering broad goals and strategic intents. The second comprises core capabilities that are integral to the delivery of products and services, or those with direct customer interaction. The third consists of capabilities that provide support to these core operational functions. This tripartite categorization echoes the structure of Michael Porter's Value Chain, a well-known concept in strategic management.

In our methodology, we have chosen not to formalize an additional overarching level (Level 0) for these categories;

instead, this is implicitly understood to exist within the structure. Should you find, however, that an explicit grouping at this preliminary level enhances the structure's clarity or utility, you are certainly allowed to do so. It's also worth mentioning that this classification can subtly guide the visual arrangement of capabilities on the CapMap; we'll explore the implications of this later.

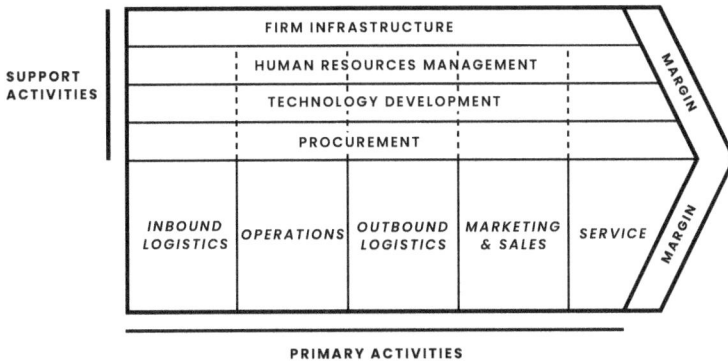

FIGURE 3.1 Michael Porter's Value Chain model [43]

Next, it is important to craft precise and comprehensive descriptions for each of the capabilities. Though the capabilities defined in this step will later be further broken down into child capabilities, clear descriptions at this level ensure that stakeholders share a common understanding of each capability's scope. This alignment is pivotal, setting the stage for fewer discrepancies when we delve into more detailed levels.

The final task in this phase is the formal validation of the structure and its descriptions. This validation is not just a formality: it ensures that, when we proceed to defining subsequent levels, we're building on a foundation of shared understanding and clarity. As mentioned earlier, you should really look at this validation of the first level as a gate to be passed through in order to move to Level 2 (phase B).

STEP B1: Deriving and defining Levels 2 and 3 + validation.
The process for developing Levels 2 and 3 of the capability
structure mirrors the initial steps, but adds a new layer of
complexity. At these levels, the primary challenge shifts from
establishing a foundational structure to determining the
degree of granularity and identifying the specific capabilities
to be included in the map. Much like in the previous phase,
achieving stakeholder consensus is still an important focus
here. As for the number of capabilities to include on each
level, there's no right answer. Personally, I advocate applying the same principle of Guiding Principle 2 to the second
level, limiting it to around 10 (plus or minus three) capabilities. This strikes a balance between detail and manageability,
ensuring the map remains a practical tool for strategic discussions and decision-making. Remember though that these
rules aren't binding, but merely guidelines to help you decide.

The challenge is in the difference in purpose
A challenge I have often encountered when defining second-
and third-level capabilities is related to those used for different purposes (such as business lines), which sometimes
means that they have very different operating models. Let's
consider, for example, the marketing capability of the Royal
BelFoot Football Club, which will have other capabilities
on the lower level, such as Campaign Management, where
campaigns target different customer segments (B2B, or
companies, versus B2C, or regular fans). In practice, these
campaigns might be developed and executed differently
between the two segments. If the differences are limited
(and the operating models quite similar), it could be that we
simply have process variations based on the segment. In this
case, the configuration of most or all operational dimensions

of the capability can remain similar for both segments, and Campaign Management remains a single capability.

However, if the capabilities truly differ in how they are organized (or should be organized according to specific profiles, which we will cover later in the chapter on Use Cases), it might make sense to split the Campaign Management capability into two child capabilities—e.g., "Campaign Management—B2B" and "Campaign Management—B2C." A situation such as this also immediately raises the question of whether it is the Campaign Management capability at this level that needs to be split, or if a higher-level split is necessary.

In such cases, the decision often comes down to ownership and performance indicators on a higher level, as well as whether the structure is similar. If both B2B and B2C campaign management contribute to the overall KPIS for campaign management, and the responsibility can be assigned to one role or person (even with separate responsibilities for B2B and B2C at a lower level), then it makes sense to keep them as separate capabilities under Campaign Management. However, if the capability structures for B2B and B2C are very different—that is, they demand different capabilities, not just different operating models for similar capabilities—it might be relevant to split them at a higher level. In most cases, this is less preferable. In figures 3.2 and 3.3 below, you will find a list of questions to help determine which three options best suit which situation.

<table>
<tr><td>

Variants (e.g. Segments)

☑ Require variants of these processes with related business logic

☑ Are processed mostly in/on the same applications

☑ Have information/data models that might differ abit, but use the same core models

☑ Roles executing the processes are the same and, if not, then they require more or less the same competencies

☑ Are assigned the same outcome for specific Use Cases, such as UC2 – Strategic Profiles

KEEP ONE CAPABILITY

</td><td>

Variants (e.g. Segments)

☑ Require separate processes, because the processing differs too much

☑ Require separate applications or truly different modules in an application

☑ Have information/data models that differ strongly

☑ Roles executing the processes are not the same and require different competencies

☑ Can not be assigned the same outcome for specific use cases, such as Use Case 2 – Strategic Profiles

SPLIT INTO MULTIPLE CAPABILITIES

</td></tr>
</table>

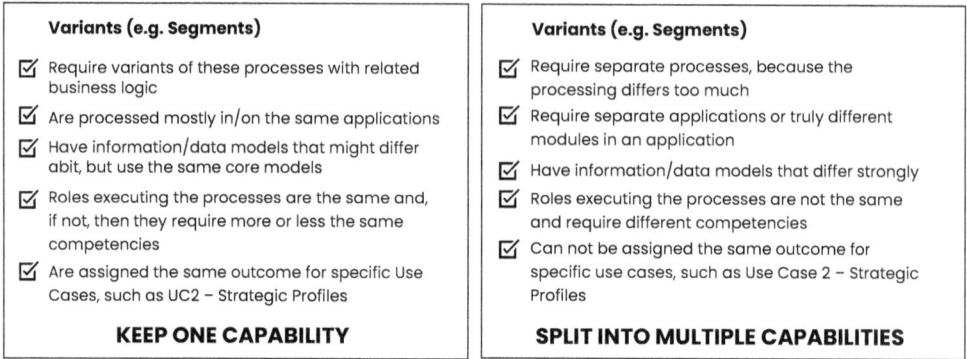

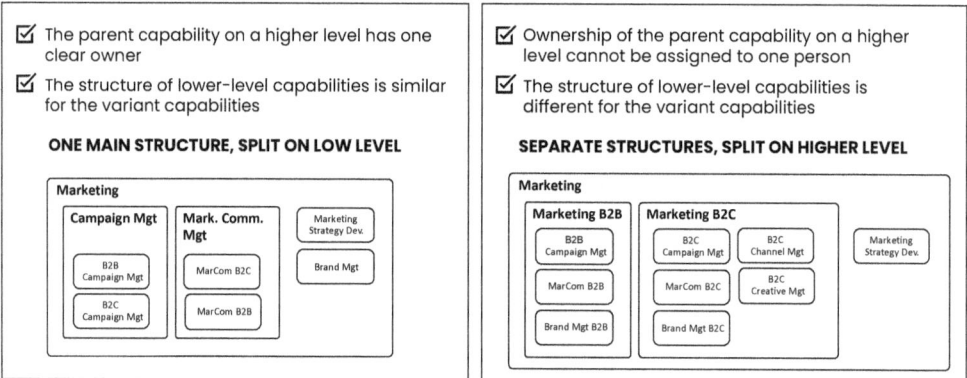

FIGURE 3.2 When to create separate variant capabilities?

SPLIT INTO MULTIPLE CAPABILITIES

FIGURE 3.3 Split variant capabilities on a lower or higher level?

A structure that reflects reality

Utilizing a reference capability structure (or CapMap, if available) can offer a significant advantage here. It provides a comprehensive checklist of capabilities that are typically relevant to organizations in a certain industry, ensuring no critical aspect is overlooked. However, it's important to rec-ognize that not all capabilities listed in a generic model may align with your organization's current objectives and scope. For example, a capability that focuses on transportation might be irrelevant if organizing transportation doesn't align with your strategic direction; or, alternatively, that transpor-tation capability may be outsourced, so it can be interesting to keep it in mind or even on the map as a relevant, but not implemented, capability. So, in other words, this disparity doesn't render these capabilities irrelevant across the indus-try, but simply indicates their current irrelevance (for now) to your specific organizational context.

The decision-making process involves defining which capabilities to incorporate into your map, as either active elements of your strategy or as absent, planned, or desired components for future consideration. Throughout this phase it's crucial to follow the guiding principles discussed above, which serve as a compass by directing the process and ensur-ing that the capability structure remains a true and effective representation of your organization's strategic framework and operational needs—in short, ensuring that the capabil-ity structure reflects the reality of the organization.

The following example shows the additional levels for the first three capabilities of the REFFS capability structure, derived in an iterative manner with multiple stakeholders. In this case, these stakeholders even came from different orga-nizations, as the goal was to create an industry reference model. But the idea stays the same: walk through the steps, define the capabilities on each of the levels together with the stakeholders, and validate before going a level deeper.

1.0 Club Strategy Management (Level 1)

1.1 Strategy Development (Level 2)

1.2 Competition Analysis (Level 2)

1.2.1 Own Market Analysis (Level 3)

1.2.2 Other Competitor Analysis (Level 3)

1.3 Trends and Market Watch and Analysis (Level 2)

1.4 Brand Strategy Development (Level 2)

1.4.1 Core Values Definition (Level 3)

1.4.2 Brand Experience Analysis (Level 3)

1.5 Innovation Management (Level 2)

1.5.1 Portfolio Management (Level 3)

2.0 Products and Services Development and Management (Level 1)

2.1 New Merchandise Development (Level 2)

2.2 New B2C Ticketing Development (Level 2)

2.3 New B2B Offering Development (Level 2)

2.4 New Sponsorship/Partnership Offering Development (Level 2)

2.5 Touchpoint Development and Management (Level 2)

3.0 Marketing and Sales Management (Level 1)

3.1 Marketing Management (Level 2)

3.1.1 Marketing Strategy Development (Level 3)

3.1.2 Marketing of Merchandise (Level 3)

3.1.3 Marketing of B2C Ticket Options (Level 3)

3.1.4 Marketing of B2B Ticket Options (Level 3)

3.1.5 Marketing of B2B Hospitality and Arrangements (Level 3)

3.1.6 Marketing of Game-day Products and Services (Level 3)

3.1.7 Marketing of B2B Sponsorship Programs (Level 3)

3.2 Brand Strategy Implementation (Level 2)

3.2.1 Branding Strategy Development (Level 3)

3.2.2 Historic Achievements/Legends (Level 3)

3.2.3 Youth Dream Development (Level 3)

3.3 Sales Management (Level 2)

3.3.1 Sales Strategy Development (Level 3)

3.3.2 Customer and Account Management (Level 3)

3.3.3 Sales Order and Contract Management (Level 3)

3.3.4 Partners and Alliances Management (Level 3)

3.3.5 Managing Omnichannel Sales (Level 3)

For the complete structure, please visit the website mentioned at the end of the book.

STEP C1: Decide on the scope, purpose, and target audience for the visual model (CapMap). As per Step A1, defining the scope is a critical first step in aligning your ambitions with the resources you have for developing a CapMap. This decision plays a pivotal role in shaping the map's effectiveness and relevance. It's important to note that various versions of the CapMap can be derived from the same foundational structure, each tailored to meet different objectives and audiences.

For instance, when a CapMap is intended for reporting to senior management or for strategic decision-making, including only the first- and second-level capabilities might be most appropriate. This keeps the focus on high-level insights, preventing the conversation from getting bogged down in too much detail. However, if the map's purpose is to align capabilities with specific processes or applications, a more detailed representation may be required. In some cases, a different format, such as a table-like structure, could be even more suitable.

Create a complete and comprehensive structure

There might also be scenarios where focusing on a specific organizational area, like logistics, is necessary. In such cases, the map would abstract from other unrelated capabilities and provide a targeted view. This flexibility highlights the importance of re-evaluating the map's purpose and scope at each stage of its development.

When resources and time allow, it's always beneficial to first develop a comprehensive and detailed capability structure that reflects most, if not all, of the organization. Such a structure provides a robust base from which various specialized CapMaps can be derived. It could be argued that if your initial focus is narrower, concentrating on a specific organizational segment may be enough. However, a word of caution: as we will explore in the Use Cases chapter, leaving out certain capabilities from the start and in the final structure (for example, supporting capabilities such as HR and IT) could lead to an incomplete understanding of their significance in achieving strategic goals.

Therefore, my recommendation is to strive for completeness in your capability structure, within the available time constraints and resources. This ensures that the various CapMaps you create, although potentially limited in scope, are grounded in a comprehensive understanding of the organization's capabilities.

STEP C2: Create and validate the visual model. The culmination of our CapMap process is the generation of the visual model itself. At this point, we must make sure we have a good view of the CapMap's intended purpose. Various perspectives of the same capability structure may be required, influenced by parameters that reflect those considered in the structuring phase. These include target audience, purpose, geographical scope, and organizational level (group, subsidiary, division etc.).

A crucial parameter to define is your target audience. For instance, when presenting to senior management, it may be prudent to abstract from Level 3 capabilities to avoid getting bogged down with detail that's too granular for the purposes of strategic focus. The map should, in that specific context, facilitate guidance and strategic decisions, necessitating a level of detail and abstraction tailored to the audience.

It's equally important to ask, "What is the CapMap's purpose?" This question considers the relevant geographical scope and organizational level, shaping the Capability Map according to the Use Cases we have in mind for it. At the end of this chapter, we will explore what different approaches for the visual model (CapMap) exist. In the next two chapters, we'll take an in-depth look at various Use Cases for Cap-Maps and how these can be applied in different scenarios.

Depending on your objectives, you may require a different level of detail or scope, or even a different form of visual representation. For example, when evaluating the IT systems supporting your logistics domain in a particular region, the scope of your map might differ significantly from one used to identify synergies during an M&A scenario. In the context of the first scenario, where a large number of IT systems might be involved, a matrix or tabular structure could prove more effective than a visual map or model. (A further word on this is coming in a following section.)

Once the model has been validated, it's time to distribute it.

STEP C3: Distribute the model. After you've developed the CapMap or any other representation of the capability structure, it's crucial to ensure that it is accessible across the organization. As per Guiding Principle 9, securing executive support is a key first step for the successful integration of the CapMap and capability structure as instrumental resources within the organization. While the utility of the model for strategic decision-making at the senior management level is already significant, wider adoption across operational levels is necessary to unlock its full potential.

In my experience, actively promoting the CapMap throughout the organization and providing targeted training for key roles on its application is highly effective. This approach empowers various organizational levels to leverage the CapMap for informed decision-making and setting up an operating model that helps to realize the strategic vision, as well as facilitating strategic alignment.

3.3   Other representations besides the CapMap

As outlined, the foundational steps in this process involve establishing the capability structure, which is a hierarchical decomposition of the organization's capabilities. Following this, the creation of the visual CapMap is undertaken. It's important, however, to recognize that for certain analytical endeavors the CapMap might not be the most suitable tool. For instance, conducting an analysis that involves listing all applications and mapping them to the capabilities they support often yields a volume of data far too extensive for a visual model that's designed to fit on a single page or slide. More crucially, incorporating such detailed information directly onto the CapMap could take away from its utility for analysis.

In scenarios like these, opting for a list or matrix structure is more advantageous. Such formats allow for the application of filters and other navigational tools, facilitating straightforward access to analytical insights. Consider, for example, assessing the impact of replacing an end-of-life application. A matrix structure simplifies the task of identifying which capabilities are associated with the specific application in question, enabling a swift and clear understanding of the functional implications.

3.4   Tools and language

Various tools are available as repositories, enabling the linkage of capabilities to other concepts like processes and applications. While these tools are intriguing and relevant, they are not our primary focus here. In my opinion, and to the best of my knowledge, no single application currently and comprehensively covers all the Use Cases detailed in this book; nor do they adequately emphasize the model over the data. As a result, in practical settings, we often resort to using PowerPoint or similar tools. PowerPoint allows for flexible modeling of capabilities and offers a broad spectrum of options for enhancing the basic CapMap with visual annotations, colors, and so on. (We'll delve deeper into these aspects in subsequent chapters.) As for the modeling languages, Archimate, for example, provides a syntax that guides the modeling effort and how to visualize the capabilities.

However, I prefer to avoid imposing rigid limitations from the outset, since my goal is to encourage you to quickly start creating CapMaps, finding a style that resonates with you and your organizational needs. The guidance provided here is just that. There is no stringent, rule-bound method to adhere to: I encourage you to adopt whatever is effective for your context, and set aside what is not.

3.5   Modeling capabilities on the CapMap

The basic shape of a capability in the map should be consistent. We can use either simple rectangles or those with rounded corners. I recommend the latter, as it allows you to distinguish capabilities from other elements like frames or sections, which can be represented with regular rectangles.

Below is an example of a modeled capability—Payroll—which encompasses the comprehensive process of managing and executing employee payment. It involves calculating wages, withholding taxes and deductions, and ensuring timely and accurate salary disbursement to all staff members. This is typically found in all organizations, but is not always internally organized (more on that later).

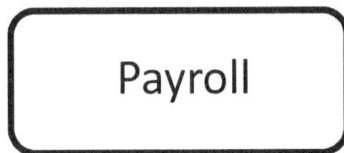

FIGURE 3.4 Example of a Capability form

Representing relationships in CapMaps

Capabilities can engage in various types of relationships with one another (for example, hierarchical relationships like parent-child, or collaborative relationships involving information exchange), as well as with other architectural elements (like information objects or processes). In this book, our primary focus is on the hierarchical relationship between parent and child capabilities, the others focusing more on the operating model. This means emphasizing the association of Level 2 capabilities with a Level 1 capability, Level 3 capabilities with a Level 2 capability, and so on. I would however advise against going further than the third level, for the sake of clarity and manageability.

The parent-child relationship in a CapMap is effectively visualized by placing lower-level capabilities within the confines of their higher-level parental counterparts. This approach is demonstrated in the image below, which shows a Level 1 capability from the REFFS structure, Product Delivery and Material Management, along with all its Level 2 and 3 child capabilities.

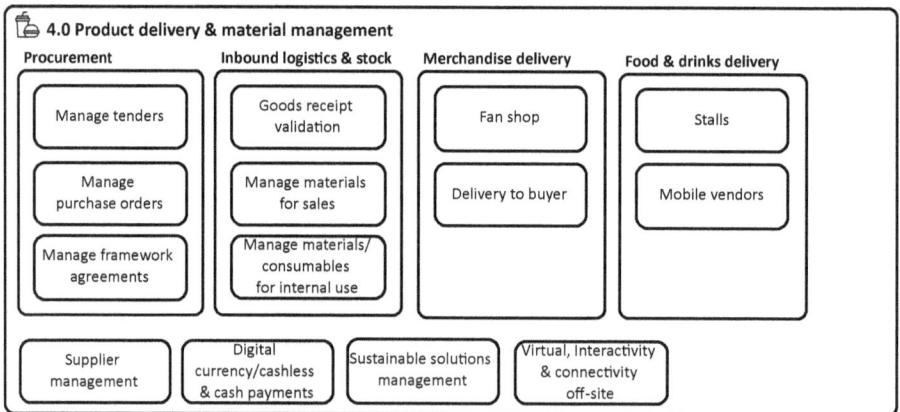

FIGURE 3.5 Example of a hierarchical structure

When it comes to shading, the choice is yours. In this example, we've applied a light grey shade for Level 2 capabilities that have Level 3 children, enhancing their visibility compared to the example above. It's important however to remember that introducing additional shades or colors could suggest some kind of further underlying logic within the model, so any such visual elements should be clearly defined and documented to avoid confusion. The use of icons (such as the burger-and-soft-drink symbol in the example below) is another modeling choice: these visual aids can quickly convey the essence of a capability to the map's reader, but their use is up to the modeler.

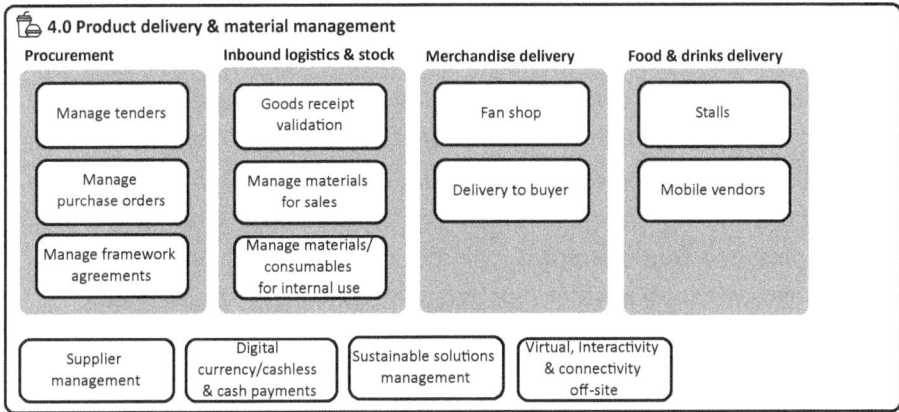

4.0 Product delivery & material management

Procurement	Inbound logistics & stock	Merchandise delivery	Food & drinks delivery
Manage tenders	Goods receipt validation	Fan shop	Stalls
Manage purchase orders	Manage materials for sales	Delivery to buyer	Mobile vendors
Manage framework agreements	Manage materials/ consumables for internal use		

Supplier management	Digital currency/cashless & cash payments	Sustainable solutions management	Virtual, Interactivity & connectivity off-site

FIGURE 3.6 Example of a hierarchical structure with shading

In textual representations of the capability structure, a hierarchical format is most effective, as exemplified in the above REFFS capability structure. This method ensures clarity and an intuitive understanding of the relationships between different levels of capabilities.

One key principle to follow, as captured in Guiding Principle 5, is that capabilities should be mutually exclusive (ME), which means that they should not be ambiguously assigned to multiple parents, either as shared responsibilities or as duplications. However, there are cases that deserve a second look. For example, I've encountered situations where a capability related to customs was argued to be a joint responsibility of both the finance and logistics departments. For me, it was the underlying processes within that capability in which multiple departments have roles or that the process can be divided in parts and needs to be decided to which capability a part can be assigned. This illustrates that when an organization can realize specific capabilities, it means that it is equally able to provide certain functions that deliver value. The fact that you explicate that the organization needs to be able to deliver these functions is one step; deciding how you will then configure your organization in practice and who will provide which functions is an operational choice. In the customs case, trying to keep the focus on the functional domain and related strategic decisions, I determined that it was best not to assign the responsibility of the capability to multiple parties, as this would leave room for finger-pointing or indecisiveness. A pragmatic solution, not a perfect one. But remember, perfection is not the goal here—usability is.

The above example illustrates both the limitations and benefits of the Capability concept. While not all processes can be perfectly boxed into a single capability, recognizing that some processes span multiple capabilities helps us focus on strategic and tactical discussions, leaving the operational complexities to be sorted out at a more granular level. Furthermore, this recognition highlights potential dependencies and complexities in operational execution, necessitating collaboration between domains. I also believe that it is best practice to try and assign accountability for a capability to one party. In cases where capabilities appear duplicated across departments, it's better to differentiate them by naming. Encountering such duplication might also be a good time to prompt a strategic review of why these similarities exist, and whether consolidating these capabilities could be advantageous.

Finally, when dealing with multiple subsidiaries that have similar capabilities, like individual HR departments, a more nuanced approach is required. We explore this scenario further in a dedicated Use Case later in the book, where we discuss strategies such as centralization versus localization to effectively manage such duplications.

3.6 Model size

In most scenarios, especially when it comes to reporting analysis findings, it's beneficial for many reasons to make the CapMap concise enough to fit on a single, landscape-format page or slide. This facilitates easy incorporation into presentations, provides a comprehensive overview of the discussion scope, and also allows for an effective comparison of different capabilities within the same visual framework.

It can however be challenging to accommodate all capabilities up to Level 3 on a single page. Therefore, it may be practical to consolidate these capabilities to the second level for reporting purposes. If detailed discussions of Level 3 capabilities are needed and a visual representation is required, consider these two approaches.

The first involves drawing all capabilities on one model, and zooming in on specific areas as needed to enlarge particular sections of the model for detailed examination. This approach maintains the integrity of the overall model but can become complex, especially depending on the software tool used. Alternatively, you can depict only the higher-level capabilities (such as Levels 1 and 2) on the main model, create detailed sub-models for specific lower-level capabilities on separate pages, and then present them as required. (In tools like PowerPoint, features like zoom-slides can be quite effective for this; other software tools may offer different functionalities, but let's focus on these two approaches for now.)

There's no uniform rule for deciding how many capabilities to showcase on the map. I advocate tailoring the model to fulfill each map's specific objectives—therefore, the inclusion of Level 2 and/or Level 3 capabilities should directly align with the insights the CapMap is designed to reveal. Additionally, it can be beneficial to explore different visual representations. For instance, aggregating detailed information into higher-level capabilities where appropriate allows for focused exploration of more granular levels, which can ensure that the map is customized for optimal strategic analysis and effective decision-making. However, adopting various views could also affect the map's immediate legibility. The key is to determine what works best for your audience *and* your organization.

3.7   Model structure and layout

As was previously emphasized, determining the scope and amount of information to display is crucial when constructing a CapMap. This decision should be guided by the map's intended purpose. Figure 3.7 (facing page) showcases a complete CapMap based on the REFFS capability structure. Note, however, that the map's layout has been adapted to fit the constraints of this book's page size. In a practical setting, how the capabilities are arranged might differ.

1.0 Club Strategy Management

Competition analysis
- Own market analysis
- Other competitor analysis

Brand Strategy Development
- Strategy development
- Trends & market watch
- Innovation management
- Portfolio management
- Core values definition
- Brand experience analysis

2.0 Products and Services development & management

Development
- Merchandise development
- B2B offering development
- Touchpoint development & management
- Sponsorship/ Partnership Offering dev.
- B2C Ticketing development

3.0 Marketing & Sales

Marketing
- Marketing strategy development
- Marketing of merchandise
- Marketing of B2C ticket options
- Marketing of B2B sponsorship programs
- Marketing of B2B hospitality and arrangements
- Marketing of gameday products and services
- Marketing of B2B ticket options

Sales management
- Sales strategy development
- Customer & account management
- Sales order & contract management
- Partners & alliances management
- Managing omnichannel sales

Brand strategy Implementation
- Branding strategy development
- Historic achievements /Legends
- Youth dream development

4.0 Product delivery & material management

Procurement
- Manage tenders
- Manage purchase orders
- Manage framework agreements
- Supplier management

Inbound logistics & stock
- Goods receipt validation
- Manage materials for sales
- Manage materials/ consumables for internal use
- Digital currency/cashless & cash payments

Merchandise delivery
- Fan shop
- Delivery to buyer

Food & drinks delivery
- Stalls
- Mobile vendors

- Sustainable solutions management
- Virtual, interactivity & connectivity off-site

8.0 IT Management
- Data & information Management
- Infrastructure Management
- Application Management
- IT Project Management

5.0 Gameday Match/Event Delivery

Physical game or event delivery
- Access control
- Accreditation/ area control
- Safety management & crowd control
- Media facilitation
- Preparing the field/pitch/venue
- Side entertainment
- Media & Big screen options
- Interactivity & connectivity on site
- Virtual delivery

Away game or event delivery
- Providing fan experience at the home venue
- Organizing away ticketing
- Organizing away transport

B2B Delivery
- Issuing tickets
- Historic achievements /Legends
- Catering
- E-sports delivery
- B2C Delivery: ticketing

6.0 Customer/Fan services and relationship

Retention & Fan engagement
- Fan engagement measurement & analysis
- Community engagement
- Loyalty program
- Fan complaints & questions handling

Touchpoint Man. & Online Presence
- Website management
- Social Media management
- Digital APP management
- Fan profile/ ID management

7.0 Staff, Player and Team Development/Management (*Duplication for women's & special interest football possible/required?)

Team performance
- Performance tracking
- Analyzing performance
- Team Training
- Opponent scouting

Player management
- Scouting
- Medical & fitness tracking
- Contract management
- Whereabouts tracking and personal guidance
- Individual Training
- Negotiation management
- Outgoing transfer management
- Whistleblower facilitation

Youth management & development
- Scouting
- Medical tracking
- Individual Training
- Guidance and education
- Training
- Whistleblower facilitation
- Medical & fitness tracking
- Contract & membership management

Volunteer management
- Safety Stewards
- Red cross/first aid
- Team representatives (youth)
- Manage other volunteers
- Matchday organization
- Ethical monitoring

- General HR Management
- Coaching staff management
- Medical & paramedical staff management
- Legal staff management

9.0 Financial Resources Management /Finance & controlling
- Cost accounting
- Forecasting
- Accounts Receivable & billing
- Accounts Payable & payments
- Payroll
- Financial Accounting & Tax Management
- Asset Accounting

10.0 Asset/Infrastructure Acquisition, Construction and Man.

Stadium management
- Pitch/field maintenance
- B2B area maintenance
- Commercial area management
- New venue/ Expansion project management
- Energy & consumables
- Seating maintenance
- Catering area management
- Other stadium activities
- Rental contract management
- Sustainability management

Training facility man.
- Training Pitch/field maintenance
- Parking maintenance and management
- Catering and leisure area management
- Rolling assets & machines
- Accessibility and traffic control

11.0 Enterprise Risk, Compliance, Remediation, and Resiliency Man.
- Risk management
- Ethical governance
- Legal & case management

Compliancy
- Regulating bodies
- Sports licensing
- Legal

12.0 External Relationships Man.
- Press Management
- Fan Clubs
- Authorities
- Academics
- Sports federations
- Referee federations
- Government
- Community
- Unions

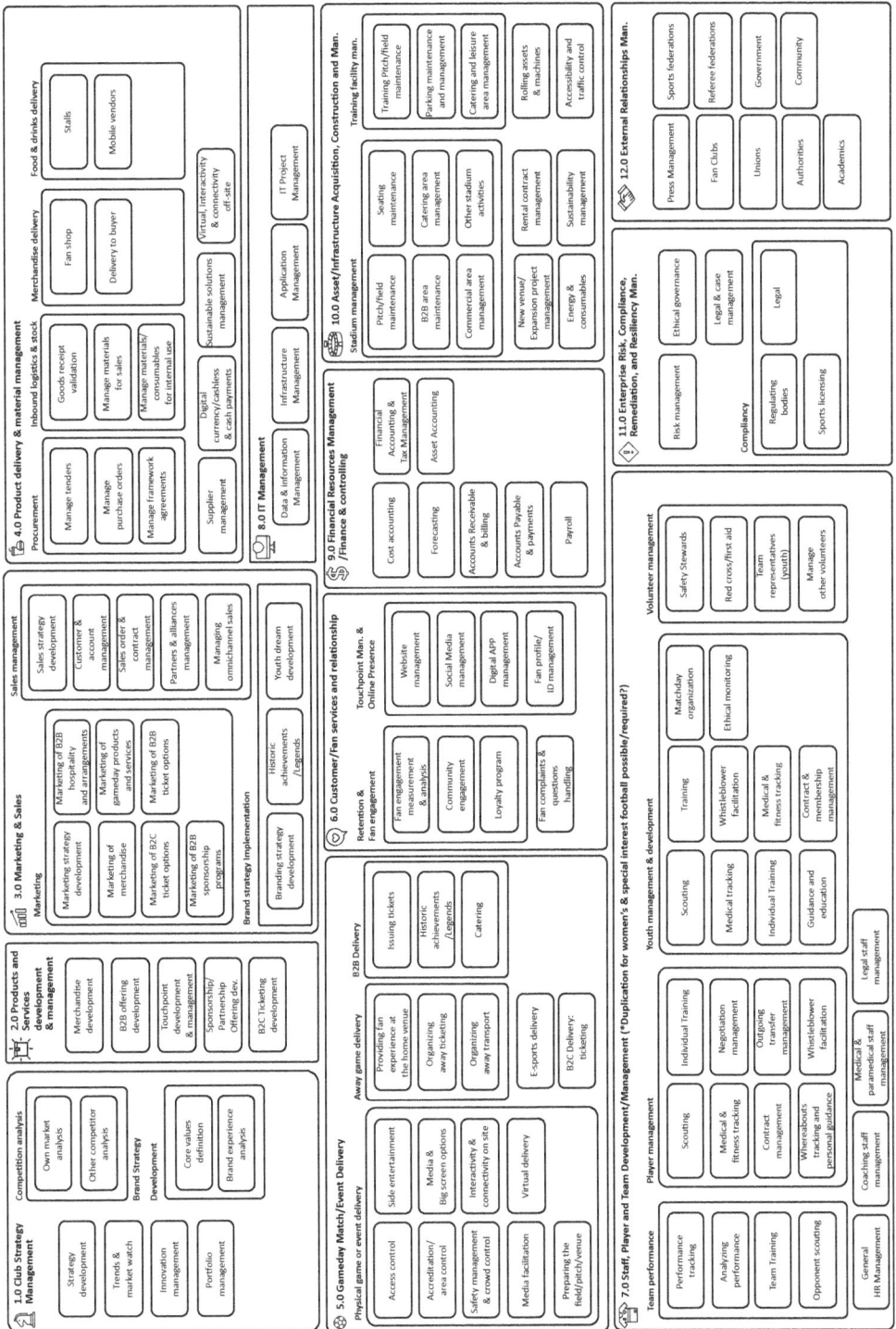

FIGURE 3.7 Complete BelFoot CapMap on one page

STRUCTURE 1: Introducing sections for supporting and primary capabilities

Adding an extra layer of structure to the CapMap can enhance its clarity and utility. As discussed earlier, incorporating a framework similar to Michael Porter's Value Chain into the CapMap's design is recommended. By doing so, supporting capabilities like HR Management, IT Management, Financial Management, etc. can be grouped together, as can the primary capabilities.

An example of a structured CapMap is shown in figure 3.8 (page 55). The key benefit of this approach is the immediate visual distinction it provides of these two types of capabilities, which often necessitate distinct strategies and approaches. This separation helps to quickly identify and focus on the different needs and management styles for different capability types. (To make the example fit on a page here, we left out the Level 3 capabilities.) Capability 2.0 and all its child capabilities could also be added to the support capabilities, but we can leave that debate for another time and place.

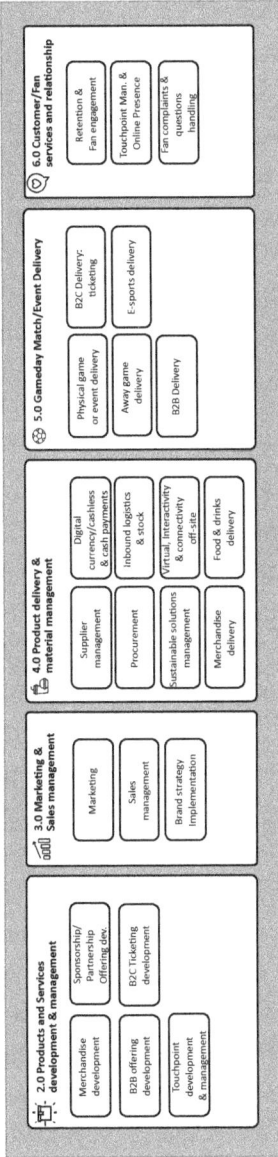

PRIMARY CAPABILITIES

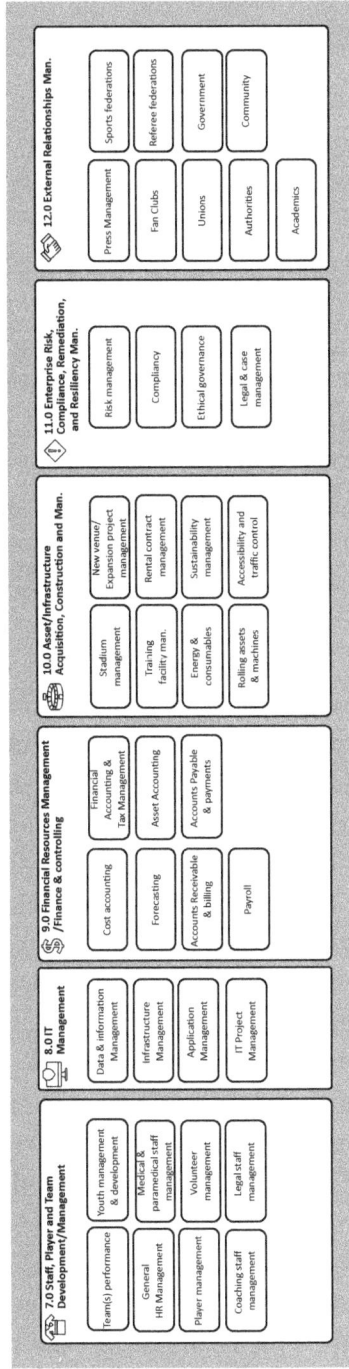

2.0 Products and Services development & management
- Merchandise development
- Sponsorship/Partnership Offering dev.
- B2B offering development
- B2C Ticketing development
- Touchpoint development & management

3.0 Marketing & Sales management
- Marketing
- Sales management
- Brand strategy Implementation

4.0 Product delivery & material management
- Supplier management
- Digital currency/cashless & cash payments
- Procurement
- inbound logistics & stock
- Sustainable solutions management
- Virtual, Interactivity & connectivity off-site
- Merchandise delivery
- Food & drinks delivery

5.0 Gameday Match/Event Delivery
- Physical game or event delivery
- B2C Delivery: ticketing
- Away game delivery
- E-sports delivery
- B2B Delivery

6.0 Customer/Fan services and relationship
- Retention & Fan engagement
- Touchpoint Man. & Online Presence
- Fan complaints & questions handling

SUPPORT CAPABILITIES

7.0 Staff, Player and Team Development/Management
- Team(s) performance
- Youth management & development
- General HR Management
- Medical & paramedical staff management
- Player management
- Volunteer management
- Coaching staff management
- Legal staff management

8.0 IT Management
- Data & information Management
- Infrastructure Management
- Application Management
- IT Project Management

9.0 Financial Resources Management /Finance & controlling
- Cost accounting
- Financial Accounting & Tax Management
- Forecasting
- Asset Accounting
- Accounts Receivable & billing
- Accounts Payable & payments
- Payroll

10.0 Asset/Infrastructure Acquisition, Construction and Man.
- Stadium management
- New venue/Expansion project management
- Training facility man.
- Rental contract management
- Energy & consumables
- Sustainability management
- Rolling assets & machines
- Accessibility and traffic control

11.0 Enterprise Risk, Compliance, Remediation, and Resiliency Man.
- Risk management
- Compliancy
- Ethical governance
- Legal & case management

12.0 External Relationships Man.
- Press Management
- Sports federations
- Fan Clubs
- Referee federations
- Unions
- Government
- Authorities
- Community
- Academics

FIGURE 3.8 BelFoot CapMap structured according to primary and support capabilities

STRUCTURE 2: Adding the strategic management section
In many organizations, a set of capabilities is specifically tied to strategic management, and recognizing these as distinct from operational capabilities offers an insightful perspective. Introducing a dedicated section for strategic management capabilities on the CapMap can therefore be highly beneficial. This section groups less tangible, more abstract capabilities that are often challenging to conceptualize operationally. Typical examples include Strategy Development, Innovation Management, Portfolio Management, and so on. Visually segregating these strategic capabilities from others underscores their unique nature and focus (as shown in figure 3.9 on the facing page).

STRUCTURE 3: Organizing core capabilities according to the customer journey
Building upon the previous structure, this last approach adds an extra dimension to the CapMap by aligning core capabilities with the customer journey. Many organizations have one or more central customer journeys that reflect a clear value stream. For instance, take a typical airline customer's journey—coming across a marketing message, searching for a flight, booking, paying, checking in, dropping off luggage, flying, onboard purchasing, claiming luggage.

In such a scenario, organizing capabilities to mirror these steps can be illuminating. Start with capabilities related to marketing, followed by those that help the search and booking processes, which are categorized as *commercial-oriented capabilities*. Then, group capabilities for check-in, luggage handling, and flight experience together as *operational capabilities*. Finally, align *customer service–related capabilities* like complaint handling together as a group.

While it is optimistic to expect a seamless fit of capabilities into such a dynamic model—given the inherently static

STRATEGIC CAPABILITIES

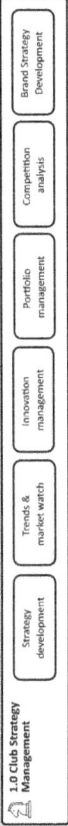

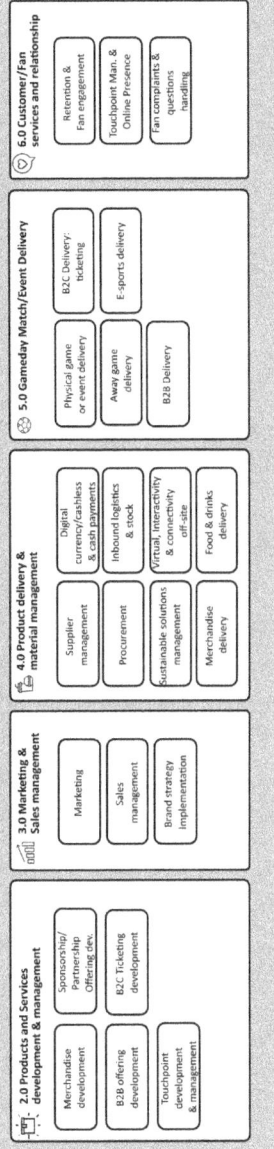

1.0 Club Strategy Management

- Strategy development
- Trends & market watch
- Innovation management
- Portfolio management
- Competition analysis
- Brand Strategy Development

6.0 Customer/Fan services and relationship

- Retention & Fan engagement
- Touchpoint Man. & Online Presence
- Fan complaints & questions handling

PRIMARY CAPABILITIES

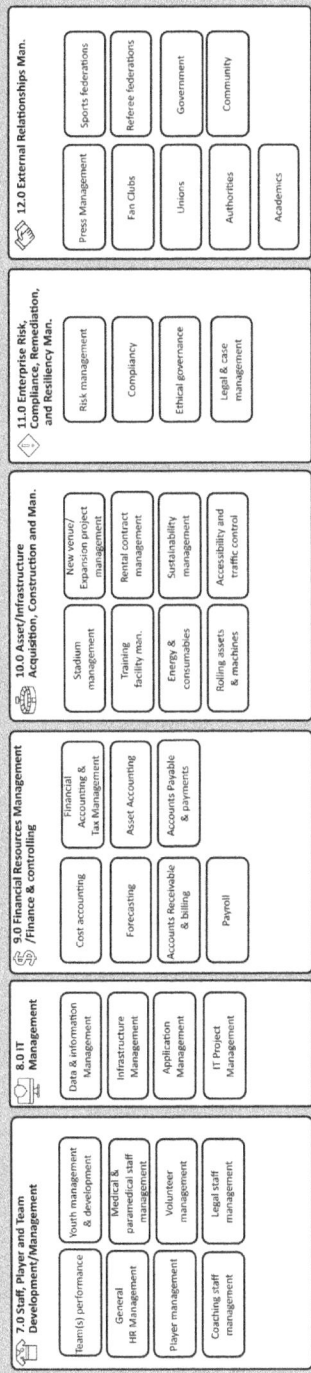

2.0 Products and Services development & management

- Merchandise development
- Sponsorship/ Partnership Offering dev.
- B2B offering development
- B2C Ticketing development
- Touchpoint development & management

3.0 Marketing & Sales management

- Marketing
- Sales management
- Brand strategy implementation

4.0 Product delivery & material management

- Supplier management
- Digital currency/cashless & cash payments
- Procurement
- Inbound logistics & stock
- Sustainable solutions management
- Virtual, Interactivity & connectivity off-site
- Merchandise delivery
- Food & drinks delivery

5.0 Gameday Match/Event Delivery

- Physical game or event delivery
- B2C Delivery: ticketing
- Away game delivery
- E-sports delivery
- B2B Delivery

SUPPORT CAPABILITIES

7.0 Staff, Player and Team Development/Management

- Team(s) performance
- Youth management & development
- General HR Management
- Medical & paramedical staff management
- Player management
- Volunteer management
- Coaching staff management
- Legal staff management

8.0 IT Management

- Data & information Management
- Infrastructure Management
- Application Management
- IT Project Management

9.0 Financial Resources Management /Finance & controlling

- Cost accounting
- Financial Accounting & Tax Management
- Forecasting
- Asset Accounting
- Accounts Receivable & billing
- Accounts Payable & payments
- Payroll

10.0 Asset/Infrastructure Acquisition, Construction and Man.

- Stadium management
- New venue/ Expansion project management
- Training facility man.
- Rental contract management
- Energy & consumables
- Sustainability management
- Rolling assets & machines
- Accessibility and traffic control

11.0 Enterprise Risk, Compliance, Remediation, and Resiliency Man.

- Risk management
- Compliancy
- Ethical governance
- Legal & case management

12.0 External Relationships Man.

- Press Management
- Sports federations
- Fan Clubs
- Referee federations
- Unions
- Government
- Authorities
- Community
- Academics

FIGURE 3.9 BelFoot CapMap, structured according to strategic, primary, and support capabilities

nature of capabilities focusing more on the "what" than on the "how" or "when"—this shouldn't scare you away from experimenting. If aligning capabilities with the customer journey enhances the utility of the CapMap, it's certainly worth exploring. Figure 3.10 (facing page) illustrates this in the case of BelFoot. Here, the customer journey has three main phases. The first focuses on marketing and selling tickets and other products, outside of game days. The second is all about delivering a good fan experience during a game day and optimizing customer value. The last phase focuses on keeping fans engaged on any other day and making sure their concerns are addressed.

3.8   Additional information

A Capability Map in its basic form—or "Base CapMap"—is an inherently valuable tool that not only signifies the culmination of a thoughtful process, but also demonstrates alignment on the fundamental "what" of an organization— i.e., its core capabilities. However, the true potential of a CapMap is unlocked when it is augmented with additional layers of information.

There are numerous ways to enrich a CapMap. The first incorporates elements like color coding to represent various insights or knowledge derived from data collection and analysis. These enhancements, explored in detail later, are referred to as "Use Cases" and "information layers," which provide deeper insights and facilitate better understanding and decision-making.

A Base CapMap can be further augmented with other related information, such as channels, customer segments, and so on. Incorporating such information can result in a more comprehensive model of the organization, making it not only holistic, but also more tangible and relevant to

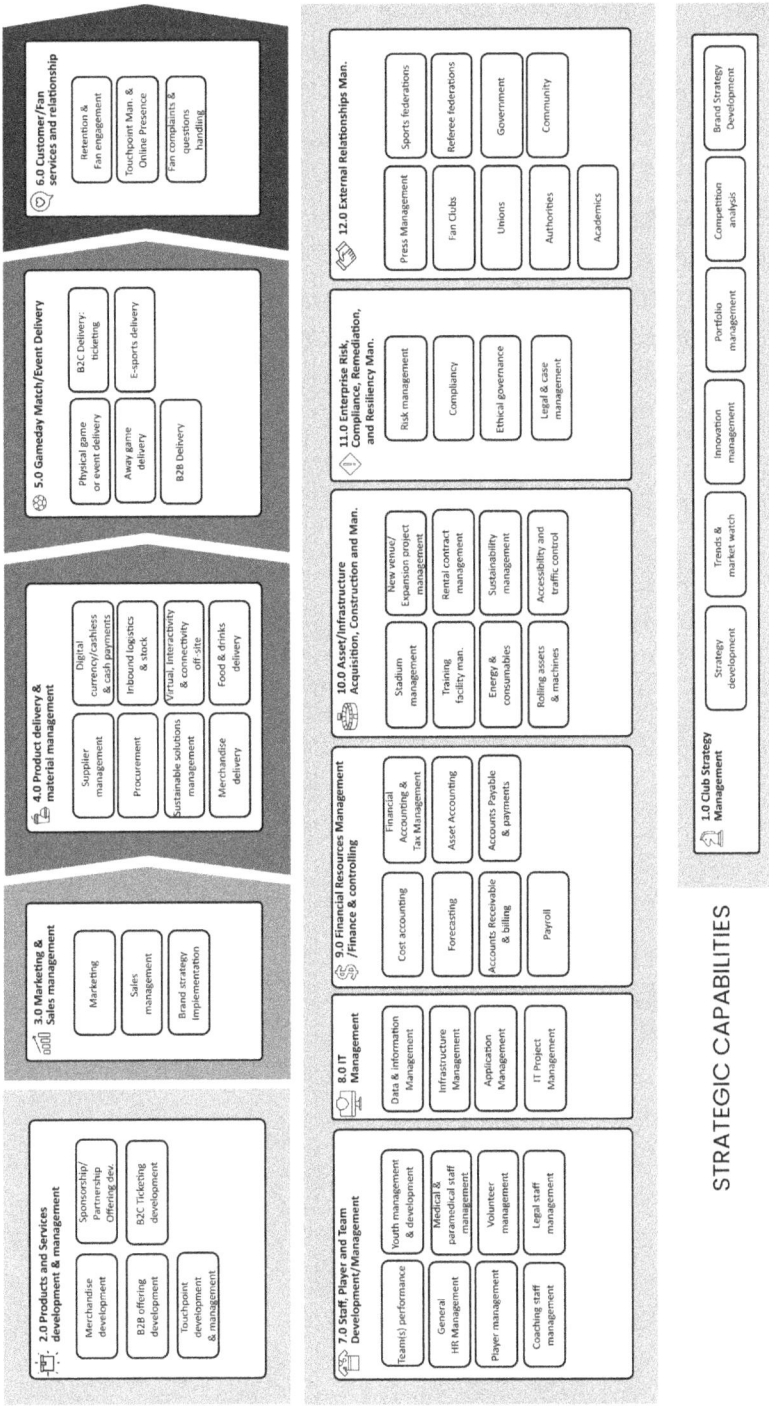

Stay Engaged

6.0 Customer/Fan services and relationship
- Retention & Fan engagement
- Touchpoint Man. & Online Presence
- Fan complaints & questions handling

Attend & Enjoy Event (Game, Food&Drinks, Merch.)

5.0 Gameday Match/Event Delivery
- Physical game or event delivery
- B2C Delivery: ticketing
- Away game delivery
- E-sports delivery
- B2B Delivery

4.0 Product delivery & material management
- Supplier management
- Digital currency/cashless & cash payments
- Procurement
- Inbound logistics & stock
- Sustainable solutions management
- Virtual, interactivity & connectivity off-site
- Merchandise delivery
- Food & drinks delivery

Discover & Buy

3.0 Marketing & Sales management
- Marketing
- Sales management
- Brand strategy Implementation

2.0 Products and Services development & management
- Merchandise development
- Sponsorship/ Partnership Offering dev
- B2B offering development
- B2C Ticketing development
- Touchpoint development & management

PRIMARY CAPABILITIES

12.0 External Relationships Man.
- Press Management
- Sports federations
- Fan Clubs
- Referee federations
- Unions
- Government
- Authorities
- Community
- Academics

11.0 Enterprise Risk, Compliance, Remediation, and Resiliency Man.
- Risk management
- Compliancy
- Ethical governance
- Legal & case management

10.0 Asset/Infrastructure Acquisition, Construction and Man.
- Stadium management
- New venue/ Expansion project management
- Training facility man.
- Rental contract management
- Energy & consumables
- Sustainability management
- Rolling assets & machines
- Accessibility and traffic control

9.0 Financial Resources Management /Finance & controlling
- Cost accounting
- Financial Accounting & Tax Management
- Forecasting
- Asset Accounting
- Accounts Receivable & billing
- Accounts Payable & payments
- Payroll

8.0 IT Management
- Data & information Management
- Infrastructure Management
- Application Management
- IT Project Management

7.0 Staff, Player and Team Development/Management
- Team(s) performance
- Youth management & development
- General HR Management
- Medical & paramedical staff management
- Player management
- Volunteer management
- Coaching staff management
- Legal staff management

SUPPORT CAPABILITIES

1.0 Club Strategy Management
- Strategy development
- Trends & market watch
- Innovation management
- Portfolio management
- Competition analysis
- Brand Strategy Development

STRATEGIC CAPABILITIES

FIGURE 3.10 BelFoot CapMap, structured according to capability types and customer journey

specific contexts. The decision to add such elements is largely up to the discretion of the modeler, in accordance with the specific objectives and circumstances in which the CapMap is being developed and utilized. I wouldn't suggest adding this additional information from the start, however, as more information might make the model difficult to understand.

CHAPTER 4

CAPABILITY-BASED MANAGEMENT (CBM)
Transforming Strategy into Action

"The pertinent question is NOT how to do things right—but how to find the right things to do, and to concentrate resources and efforts on them."

PETER F. DRUCKER

4.1 What is it?

In today's rapidly changing business and digital transformation landscape, the capacity to convert strategic visions into tangible plans is crucial. Bridging the gap between strategic ambitions and operational realities is a significant challenge that many management theories have sought to address.

In the 1990s, renowned strategy authors Robert Kaplan and David Norton highlighted the limitations of focusing solely on financial perspectives, advocating for a more balanced and holistic approach in the Balanced Scorecard.

They extended their methodology to Strategy Maps, which aim to delineate cause-effect relationships and clarify drivers behind strategic ambition realization in their books [19, 20]. While Strategy Maps are a powerful tool (and absolutely innovative when originally conceived), when it comes to allowing organizations to improve their strategic processes I believe they still fall short of providing a direct framework for detailing decisions related to the operating model across various domains (or capabilities, as we've termed them). Although this step is not totally ignored, the approach doesn't provide sufficient handles and guidance to execute it.

This gap is where Capability-Based Management (CBM) becomes invaluable. CBM aims to gather and present analytical insights to synchronize strategic ambitions with an organization's capabilities, offering a structured and actionable framework that effectively closes this gap and elevates Strategy Maps. High-level strategic discussions, such as priority-setting, are distilled into actual decisions and represented on the CapMap—decisions which can then serve as guiding principles moving forward to operating-model planning.

Implementing and executing strategy often requires transforming the organization, and relies heavily on a robust change management strategy. As Nitin Nohria and Michael Beer point out in an article for the *Harvard Business Review* [21], around 70% of change initiatives fail, often because managers become overwhelmed by various recommendations and lose focus and clarity. The article highlights two primary theories of change: Theory E, which focuses on economic value through measures like downsizing and restructuring; and Theory O, which centers on organizational capability and cultural development. While both have merits, each also carries significant costs. Finding a balance between the two is challenging, but essential for sustainable success.

For me, Capability-Based Management provides a structured approach to address these challenges. It acts as a bridge between strategy and operations, enabling better transformations and facilitating bottom-up input, leading to grounded decisions and the creation of fitting capabilities. Through CBM, organizations can better integrate the hard economic focus of Theory E with the soft cultural focus of Theory O, achieving a balanced, effective approach to change that enhances both shareholder value and organizational capability.

Looking to the future

By now, you'll understand that the concept of (business or enterprise) capability lies at the core of CBM—it's a central component of Enterprise Architecture (EA) that CBM seeks to amplify, as explained in the previous chapters. CBM involves a comprehensive set of activities—planning, organizing, actuating, and controlling—all aimed at achieving predefined objectives. By focusing on a capability-based structure for decision-making, CBM offers a methodical approach for steering through organizational transformations and aligning management efforts with future directions.

The primary instrument in CBM is the capability structure and its visual representation—the CapMap—which offer a structured and hierarchical view of an organization's capabilities. In the practice of CBM, the CapMap becomes a foundational baseline for evaluating the impact and feasibility of strategic initiatives, supporting new strategy formulation, analyzing capability changes, and planning the transformation journey essential for strategy implementation and, eventually, strategy execution. This book explores multiple Use Cases of the CapMap, each requiring the gathering and analysis of different information to answer the questions of the strategic management and operational management team.

4.2   The core Use Cases of CBM

Capability-Based Management acts as a comprehensive framework for tackling a wide range of management challenges and scenarios, with digital transformations being a prime example. As we've seen, while the CapMap and its development process inherently offer substantial value, its true utility and value are realized when the map reflects a story extending far beyond simply documenting the functional domains of an organization. This multifaceted application of the CapMap is what truly distinguishes it as a tool, these different applications being categorized and described in this book as various "Use Cases."

However, while the CapMap is the most important model for CBM and will be the standard representation option in this book, in some cases the CapMap might not be the best visual model for the Use Case and what we aim to achieve. Such situations will better benefit from using a different visual representation, such as the matrix format, which will be clearly indicated in the explanation and description of each case.

Now, what exactly do we mean when we talk about "Use Cases"? Use Cases, as a common tool in IT system analysis and design, for example, provide a structured explanation of how specific solutions (such as systems, techniques, or models) are applied. The objective of detailing Use Cases is threefold: first, to capture the intended goals; second, to pinpoint the actors involved; and third, to elaborate on the functionality and context of the solution's deployment. For this book, the term "Use Case" is applied for the similar way in which the relevant information, in terms of the CapMap's different practical applications, is documented. The concept of a CBM Use Case is illustrated in figure 4.1 (below), where the outcome of a specific analysis is mapped onto the Cap-Map, enriching it with an additional layer of information.

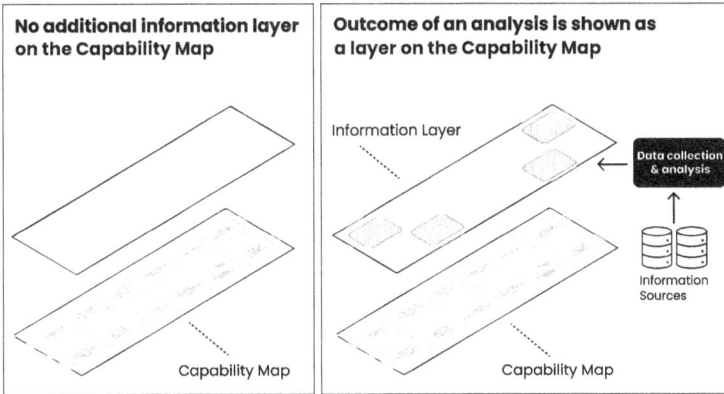

FIGURE 4.1   Layers on a CapMap

The CapMap as a canvas for decision-making

This book presents two distinct types of Use Cases. For each, you will find details on the data gathered and analyzed, and an illustration of how the outcomes of these analyses are visually represented on the CapMap. The first type delves into the inquiries the CapMap facilitates, and emphasizes the CapMap's functionalities and its potential as a versatile platform or tool for generating insights and interpretations at a strategic level. Its primary goal is to establish the CapMap as a fundamental tool in strategic decision-making, high-lighting its role in synthesizing and visualizing critical data.

As an example, plot performance data on the domains to help an organization decide where it needs to improve and invest. Gathering the information related to this per-formance is done via other methods. The information itself is then plotted on the CapMap, which then functions as the central canvas to draw insights from.

Decisions that guide

Use Cases of the second type, meanwhile, aim to display the outcome of an analysis on the CapMap in the form of concrete decisions. These then serve as guiding principles for translating strategic ambitions and decisions towards the organization and its operating model. They follow a more directive approach, demonstrating how the CapMap can be dynamically employed to facilitate decision-making processes at a lower (operating) level. In these cases, the CapMap becomes a powerful tool for communicating and promoting strategic decisions throughout the organization— an important part of strategy implementation.

As an example, plot out decisions relating to outsourcing. When the strategic decision is to outsource specific capabilities, indicate this on the CapMap to provide a clear direction for those that need to shape capabilities in practice by configuring resources into the proper operating model. It also helps to define programs and projects based on this information.

(Note that the examples of both types of Use Cases above are obviously simplified; those covered later in this chapter will be more realistic and explained in more detail.)

4.2.1   USE CASE 0: Maturity Levels

I refer to this as "Use Case 0" because it reflects a foundational element for managing capabilities and can help to effectively execute other Use Cases. Assessing the maturity level of a capability provides a structured way of evaluating how well it is managed. This concept is similar to Business Process Management (BPM), where processes are assigned various "maturity" levels that typically range from 0 or 1 (unmanaged) to 5 (highly managed, characterized by performance measurement and continual optimization) [22]. Using these maturity levels offers a systematic approach to evaluating and improving an organization's CBM maturity. The levels span from "Initial" to "Optimized," with each step representing an increased capacity to manage and enhance capabilities effectively. These maturity levels are invaluable for setting management expectations for each capability, which then informs the requirements for other Use Cases.

The classic maturity levels are:

1   **LEVEL 1: Ad Hoc/Initial**. The capability exists, but there are no formal roles or processes established.

2   **LEVEL 2: Repeatable/Managed**. The capability is managed at a basic level, with some consistency in process execution, but without formal documentation.

3   **LEVEL 3: Defined and Documented**. The organization has a clear understanding of how the capability should operate. The operating model (including processes, roles, and supporting applications) is documented, but not all operational details need to be included. While goals may be defined, there is no systematic measurement of performance indicators, making this a largely reactive stage. The key processes that require monitoring and control must also meet this maturity level, but from a BPM point of view.

4   **LEVEL 4: Measured and Controlled**. The capability is actively monitored, with performance indicators and controls in place. The organization takes corrective actions as needed to maintain performance, reflecting a more proactive management approach. The key processes that need to be measured and controlled need to be up to this level as well.

5   **LEVEL 5: Continuous Optimization**. The capability is subject to ongoing monitoring and data analysis, with continual improvements being designed and implemented based on performance insights, reflecting a higher level of proactivity.

Not all capabilities need to be managed at the highest maturity level—in fact, Level 5 is rarely necessary, or even feasible. The appropriate maturity level depends on factors such as the (strategic) importance of the capability and the context in which it operates. For example, capabilities critical to the organization's core offerings may require Level 4 or 5 management to ensure optimal performance. Conversely, capabilities that are not strategically significant or are in early stages of innovation might operate effectively at a lower maturity level, allowing for greater flexibility and rapid iteration.

Additionally, not all operational dimensions within a capability—such as business processes—need to achieve the same level of maturity. It is possible, for instance, for a capability to be generally considered at Level 1, while certain key processes within it operate at a higher level. Conversely, a capability might aim for Levels 4 or 5, but not all its processes will require such a high maturity level. Therefore, a capability is considered to reach a specific level when the processes, roles, and other elements that need to meet that level have done so. For instance, if processes X and Y need to be at Level 4, the capability can only be considered to have achieved it once these processes have met the necessary criteria. However, even though reflecting on the current and required maturity level of the capabilities of an organization is valuable and relevant, it does not mean that other Use Cases cannot be applied before this reflection has been done.

4.2.2   USE CASE 1: Strategic Emphasis through Motivation Modeling

If everything is a priority, then nothing is

On August 17, 2023, part of the quote of the day on McKinsey's website read: "If everything is a priority, then nothing is." I have personally echoed this sentiment for the last decade. Ask a senior management team about their priorities for the next two years, and it's likely each C-suite member will have a divergent focus, all deemed equally critical by the people advocating them.

For a middle manager, few challenges are as daunting as operating effectively without clarity on overarching priorities. So, one of the most critical tasks for senior management, beyond outlining the business model and commercial strategy, is answering this pivotal question: "What do we aim to achieve as an organization?" This may seem straightforward, but it's often not. Its significance stems from its role as a prerequisite to discerning "Which capabilities should we acquire, change, reinforce, or dispose of to realize our strategic ambitions?" This is inherently tied to a Fit-Gap analysis, allowing us to envisage the future state of each capability, which is closely linked to the question posed in Chapter 2: "Which capabilities make your firm unique today—and which will in the future?" [10]. However, focusing only on the uniqueness of specific capabilities might lead us to overlook others that might be crucial to driving success. So, for me, the real question is: "What capabilities, and in what form, are most critical to securing and maintaining our valuable competitive position?" [9]. Answering this question demands deeper insights and necessitates further analysis. The various Use Cases of CBM outlined here are designed to provide multiple valuable insights, offering a robust framework for analyzing and optimizing capabilities essential for sustaining competitive advantage.

Outcome-oriented

Feeling overwhelmed by this challenge is natural, as you need to integrate a lot of information to answer several crucial questions. Strategic orientation is complex and laden with assumptions and estimates that lack certainty. However, CBM provides a structured approach to this challenge, starting not with the CapMap but with the capabilities defined within. The analysis for this Use Case isn't done on the CapMap, but it makes use of the defined capabilities. And, as our first Use Case, it's a prescriptive one in which we will plot the outcome of the analysis on the CapMap and thus allow it to serve as a guiding principle for later analysis and decisions.

I call this Use Case "Strategic Emphasis through Motivation Modeling" because we need to discern which capabilities are critical for fulfilling strategic ambitions. Does this imply neglect for the rest? Absolutely not. However, given limited resources, our focus must initially gravitate towards what matters most ("finding the right things to do"). This process, known as "goal derivation" or "motivation modeling," starts from organizational targets and ambitions. These are often broadly defined, which contributes to the difficulty of translating them into operational reality. By translating vision and mission statements into tangible goals and targets, we pinpoint the capabilities that become strategic enablers.

While methodologies such as the Business Motivation Model (BMM) by the Object Management Group (OMG) [23] and the motivation and strategy concepts (e.g., drivers, goals, courses of action, value stream, capabilities) from the Archimate language provide extensive frameworks for goal derivation, and good examples have been published [24], this book adopts a more pragmatic approach. Those seeking in-depth knowledge on the subject may explore the breadth of possibilities these frameworks offer, but in this book you will find an alternative approach which aims to be pragmatic and widely applicable.

In the introduction to Chapter 2, we established that an organization must strike a balance between its desired identity (mission), its aspirational endpoint (vision and what the market/environment demands), and the capabilities required to actualize these aims. This balancing act ideally commences with an integration of the mission, vision, and market influences into the business strategy, outlining our market offerings, target demographics, and geographic focuses. However, as Kaplan and Norton have shown, our perspective must transcend the financial and commercial aspects of the organization. We must also explore other drivers, such as legal and internal drivers. Bridging our vision with operational reality necessitates intermediate steps that will, in turn, pinpoint the capabilities essential for driving its realization. After all, it might not seem obvious at first, but multiple capabilities can (and will) contribute to the realization of this vision and the successful implementation (and execution) of the business model. Furthermore, we will often find that supporting capabilities, such as HR- and IT-related ones, will be deemed crucially important. With this in mind, we will now delve into the four steps of the strategic orientation process that form the basis of this first Use Case of Capability-Based Management.

The analysis steps

STEP 1: **Identifying drivers.** The journey begins with the organization's vision and mission. From there, we need to understand what drives that organization towards its vision. However, it's not just about identifying these drivers, but also understanding their "why." This is an important part of strategic orientation—diving into the layers of each driver to reveal its contribution to the vision's realization. By deconstructing drivers into more nuanced sub-drivers, we grasp the subtleties that dictate our strategic direction. To put it another way, each sub-driver is a strand in a complex web of organizational motivation that, when pulled, reveals the contours of our future goals.

The example opposite helps illustrate the steps in this process. In addition to what is shown here, you could also add stakeholders and assessments of the drivers to better illustrate why the goals are defined. (Again, more specialized resources are available for those looking to dive deeper into this subject.)

Let's return to our fictional football club, Royal BelFoot. Club leadership, as with the strategic decision-making of any organization, must determine the club's identity and pinpoint growth opportunities.

Imagine that Royal BelFoot shares its city with a rival club, competing in the same league. This other club not only contends with Royal BelFoot on the pitch, but also vies for the same fan base and sponsorship revenues. Analysis shows that, whereas this competitor capitalizes on a grittier image and draws income primarily through sporting triumphs and associated sponsorships, Royal BelFoot chooses a different path. The club aspires to cultivate a family-oriented environment, aiming to forge long-term alliances with organizations that value nurturing customer and business relationships in an engaging and congenial setting.

At the heart of this strategic pivot is fan satisfaction. Take a look at the image below and reflect on how the key driver is divided into more detailed drivers.

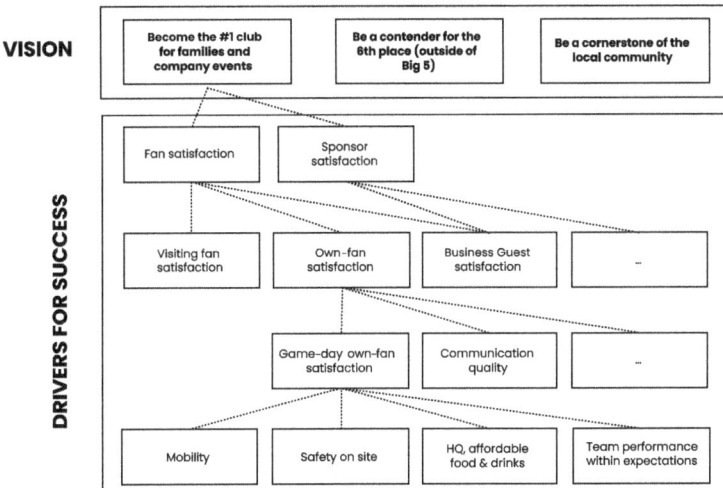

This case study narrows its scope to a segment of the strategic vision, specifically focusing on the mobility driver, to avoid excessive complexity. However, a truly comprehensive analysis must extend to other drivers, assessing which are most pivotal and what specific goals or targets should be established. The rest of the case is presented below, after an explanation of the other steps.

STEP 2: Defining goals. Once we've laid bare the drivers, we need to turn them into concrete, tangible goals—the step where the abstract becomes actionable. Goals must be articulated with precision—they must be clear, measurable, and time-bound. Setting targets with percentages or numbers not only brings specificity to our objectives, but also readies the organization for a transformation that's both measurable and achievable. These goals become signposts, guiding us through a fog of strategic ambiguity to the clarity of a defined destination.

STEP 3: Articulating requirements. Goals now in hand, at this step we have to ask ourselves: "What is required to reach them?" This stage is about translating goals into requirements, the building blocks of our strategic initiatives. Requirements are the bridge between the "what" of our goals and the "how" of our capabilities. They distill our ambitions into components that will later inform the structure and operations of our enterprise.

STEP 4: Identifying key capabilities. This step involves discerning the crucial capabilities to fulfil and implement the set requirements. This marks a pivotal point—one where we obtain a clear picture of which capabilities are essential for bringing our strategic vision and ambitions to life. It's important to note that it's often the supporting capabilities that prove to be fundamental in achieving specific objectives, and these can be inadvertently underestimated.

Take, for example, the capabilities of a Project Management Office (PMO). If it's determined that the organization must undertake significant changes, this heralds a comprehensive organizational transformation that encompasses numerous projects. The successful management of such a portfolio of projects necessitates robust PMO capabilities. Similarly, when the aim is to refine certain capabilities for cost efficiency—such as applying lean or Six Sigma methodologies in production— the Business Process Management (BPM) capability assumes greater significance. Therefore, it's imperative to extend our analysis beyond the apparent capabilities and diligently seek to identify all capabilities that will be impacted.

While tangible goals enable the crafting of definitive requirements to achieve
our aims, it's acceptable to start with a higher-level, more abstract approach
and refine the specifics later. In our Royal BelFoot example, concrete targets
are identified, necessitating the commercial development, marketing, and
sales of new mobility services. Study the image below, where we continue the
analysis and identify goals, requirements, and impacted capabilities.

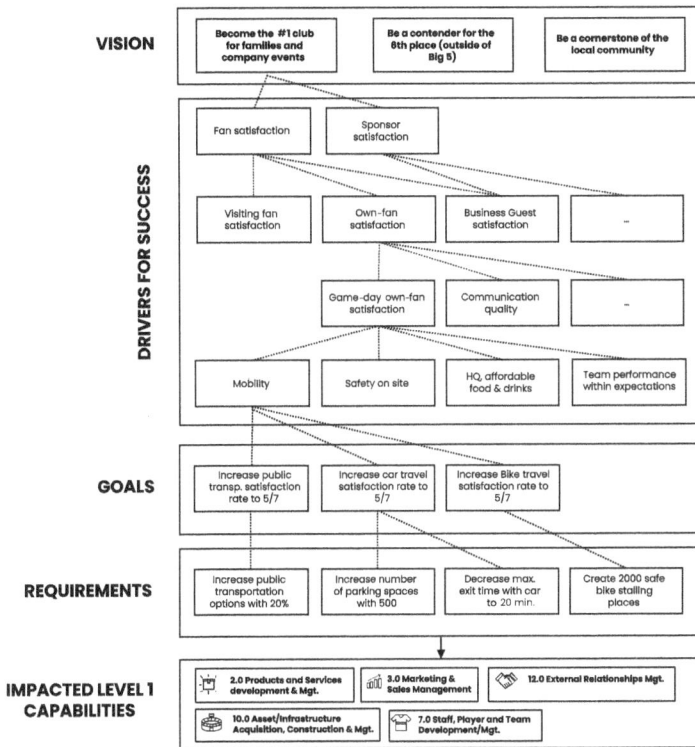

Other impacted key capabilities here include volunteer management—a sub-
set of Staff, Player, and Team Development/Management—and the management of external relationships. The cultivation of robust connections with law
enforcement and the facilitation of partnerships for parking space rentals are
also identified as vital. Additionally, on-site parking development and secure
bicycle storage highlights the importance of the Asset/Infrastructure capability.

For visual clarity, the example above is restricted to Level 1 capabilities,
and I have not explicitly linked these requirements to goals; in practice, however, it's advantageous to delve into the more granular, lower-level capabilities when feasible. Nonetheless, this example still provides significant detail.
Should you need to perform an initial estimation of potential impact areas,
keeping it simple can offer an early directional guide and stimulate the necessary strategic dialogues.

Indicating strategic emphasis on the CapMap

The illustration below offers an in-depth example of the motivational model in action, showcasing practical application of the steps. The primary goal of this initial deployment of Capability-Based Management is to identify leverage points for potential improvement or change. Once key capabilities critical to achieving our strategic vision are identified—these being the cornerstone of our success—they should be distinctly marked on the CapMap.

A clear method is to delineate these capabilities with an extra-bold border. For a more nuanced approach, employing numerical indicators (e.g., 1-2-3) at the corners of each capability block can indicate varying priorities or connections to strategic drivers (as in our example case, where capabilities linked to different drivers might be tagged accordingly without suggesting a hierarchy). Figure 4.2 illustrates how this might be done in practice.

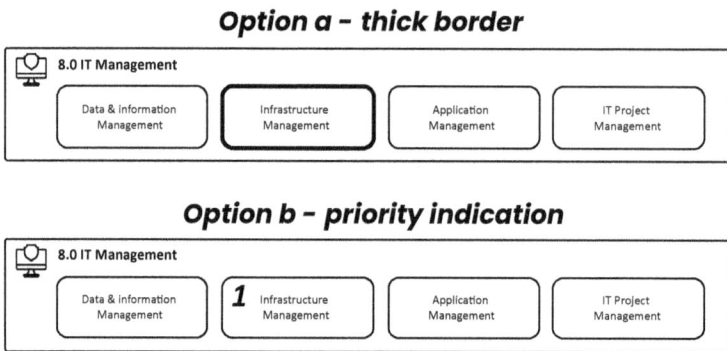

Option a - thick border

Option b - priority indication

FIGURE 4.2 Strategic emphasis indicated
on the CapMap—two possible options

Nevertheless, caution is advised here, in two respects. First, an overabundance of capabilities marked as strategically important may signal the need to reassess and prioritize goals. There can't be too many priorities, because then none stand out.

Second, visually linking capabilities to all drivers on the same CapMap could lead to a cluttered and confused presentation, potentially diminishing clarity. If there are multiple drivers all linked to multiple capabilities, we get a lot of information on the map. An alternative approach could be to generate separate views for each principal driver, displaying related capabilities for each. Then, as a summarized view, we can again amalgamate them into an integrated overview. Ultimately, it's up to the analyst to tailor the CapMap in consideration of its purpose and target audience.

Some reflections

The strategic team, often bolstered by external consultants, is tasked with determining the drivers and their priority, and then assigning appropriate goals. Note that setting a goal does not inherently imply improvement of the linked capabilities—at times, the aim may be to sustain a current performance level. This could necessitate either preserving existing capabilities, or fortifying them in anticipation of future requirements to ensure consistency in performance. As you know, we need to further analyze to find an answer to these questions (and Use Cases 2 and 3 will help us do so). However, in many cases, the approach taken to indicate goals and related impact might differ from that presented here. That's fine, if the strategic emphasis is somehow translated towards the impacted capabilities and visually illustrated on the CapMap.

It is also pertinent to acknowledge that this initial approach solely concentrates on potential areas of interest, irrespective of actionable possibilities. This implies that after applying the analysis methods presented in the subsequent

Use Cases, you will probably need to revisit this phase. For example, the Fit-Gap analysis presented in Use Case 3 may reveal that it's impossible to focus on and execute actions for all intended goals, because it would mean that you have too much to change all at once as an organization. This can be viewed as harmonizing the entrepreneurial approach (focused on what we aspire to achieve and envisioning limitless possibilities) with a more pragmatic, realistic, military-like approach that considers what's achievable with the resources available.

CBM Use Case 1—Strategic Emphasis through Motivation Modeling

Type: Prescriptive

Description: Based on the organization's strategic goals and ambitions, a cause-effect relationship model is created. This model identifies the capabilities that are strategically important for realizing these ambitions. In other words, it highlights the primary focus capabilities that contribute to achieving the goals.

The purpose is to provide a scope for further analysis, streamlining the effort, and presenting a first idea to leadership of how to allocate the project budget (CAPEX) and provide a first focus for portfolio management. If the strategic goals and ambitions are unclear or misaligned, attempting to apply this Use Case will make it explicit. Without well-defined goals and ambitions, it is impossible to identify the most relevant capabilities needed to achieve them.

Audience: Multiple stakeholders, e.g., Senior Management (C-suite), Board of Directors, Middle Management.

Main facilitator: External consultant (facilitator) or internal analysts (Strategic Analyst, Enterprise Architect), with input from key stakeholders (Leadership Team, Senior IT Manager, Enterprise Architects).

What main actions are needed? Interviewing the stakeholders, facilitating workshops, creating the goal derivation model, indicating emphasis on the map.

Information captured: A "status" is assigned to the capabilities indicating whether a capability is essential for achieving strategic ambitions. This status is determined by using goal motivation techniques, or other techniques such as Strategy Mapping.

Information plotted on CapMap: Capabilities are assigned a thick border or numeric priority value to indicate their importance.

Preconditions: A Capability Map should be present and accepted by the different parties. Strategic goals/ambitions should be clear and aligned.

4.2.3   USE CASE 2: Strategic Profiles for Capabilities

The work of Michael Porter

The initial Use Case is valuable for identifying capabilities considered crucial to the realization of your vision and which deserve further analysis to determine their current state. To do this, however, we first need to decide what is expected of these capabilities (in terms of operating model and output) at a high level. A good starting point is to decide how capabilities will best serve the realization of the organization's strategic vision, taking into account what the desired market position should be.

This next Use Case is aptly titled "Strategic Profiles for Capabilities," highlighting the significance of identifying which capabilities facilitate, for example, business differentiation, and which ones may be considered commodities within the industry. With this in mind, let's take a step back and revisit Michael Porter's strategic framework, as described in his 1980 work [44], which outlines three generic strategies for achieving competitive advantage: cost leadership, differentiation, and focus.

Michael Porter's strategies for competitive advantage

Cost Leadership: This strategy involves the company becoming the lowest-cost producer in its industry. Cost leaders typically sell a standard, no-frills product and emphasize efficiency and cost reduction at every level. Companies that effectively implement this strategy can earn above-average returns even when the industry is faced with strong competitive forces.

Differentiation: With this strategy, a company seeks to be unique in its industry in dimensions widely valued by customers. This is often achieved by creating a product or service perceived as exclusive or superior. This differentiation might come from the brand image, proprietary technology, customer service, features, etc. The key is that customers must be willing to pay more for these unique attributes.

Focus: The focus strategy is about targeting a specific niche segment of the market and serving it better than anyone else. This focus can be driven by cost (being the low-cost option within that niche) or differentiation (offering a product or service within that niche that is distinct). The focus strategy is often used by smaller companies with limited resources, but it can also be employed by larger companies targeting specific market segments.

Porter asserts that strategies can be mixed to achieve competitive advantage, although he cautions against mixing too much as this would risk leaving a company "stuck in the middle" and lacking a clear competitive stance. My main reservation with Porter's model is that it leans too heavily towards market-focused strategies, often suggesting a one-size-fits-all approach that oversimplifies the multifaceted nature of organizations and somewhat ignores the internal operations. However, I believe the model's true value lies in its relation and translation towards the Capability concept. I applaud the definition of a market strategy where an organization decides how it should position itself in the market compared to competitors—for both their products and, importantly, all other customer-facing services and products, such as customer after-sales services. Focusing solely on the product side would mean ignoring a large part of your value chain, so it makes sense to include all value-creating capabilities in this equation.

However, I believe this decision needs further fine-tuning and should not be limited to the primary activities of the value chain. I will therefore continue diving a little deeper into this problem. First, though, let's take the discussion onto the capability level and then include all capabilities in the conversation, including those linked to an organization's support activities.

Gartner's Pace Layer model comes into play

Examining the implications at the capability level, the importance of strategic choices in how capabilities should be operated becomes evident. But the actual link between Porter's framework and the choices on a capability level demand further examination. Gartner's Pace-Layered Application Strategy is pertinent to this discussion. Gartner posits that organizations need a nuanced strategy for business applications, one that aligns with their ambition to leverage technology not only for establishing long-term differentiation, but also for fostering innovative processes—and all the while maintaining a secure and cost-efficient support structure for core business operations.

The three tiers suggested by Gartner—spanning common, different, and innovative operational approaches—are particularly insightful. These can be seen as levels of standardization, differentiation, and innovation, each benchmarked against market or industry norms. According to Gartner, the selection among these approaches significantly influences the design and functionality of business applications.

The first tier, standardization, gives rise to *Systems of Record*—robust systems that are selected for their stability, efficiency, and reliability in supporting processes and managing data. Due to their need for high reliability, they are inherently resistant to too much change, and are typically acquired off-the-shelf rather than being custom-built. However, while they are foundational, such systems don't confer a competitive edge in themselves.

The second tier, differentiation, ushers in *Systems of Differentiation*. As the name suggests, these systems are adaptable, and allow for the modification of business logic and rules to provide a unique market stance.

The final tier, innovation, leads to *Systems of Innovation*. Designed for agility and prioritizing the rapidity of change over other qualities like execution efficiency and reliability, these are often essential attributes of more established systems [45].

A more detailed overview of each of these tiers follows:

Gartner's Pace Layers

Systems of Record: These core systems support fundamental transaction processing and manage the organization's critical master data. The rate of change is slow, and functionality more or less standardized across industries. Examples include ERP systems, inventory management, and accounting software.

Systems of Differentiation: These applications enable unique company processes or industry-specific capabilities. They have a moderate rate of change, and are usually tailored to the needs of the business or industry. Examples include customer relationship management (CRM) systems, or supply chain management systems customized to provide a competitive advantage.

Systems of Innovation: These systems are typically new applications built on an ad hoc basis to address new business requirements or opportunities. They have a high rate of change, and are typically short-lived (they may be replaced entirely as business needs evolve). Examples include mobile applications, digital marketing platforms, or experimental IoT projects.

Strategic Profiles for Capabilities and operating-model dimensions

Attentive readers will recognize that focusing solely on applications is a rather narrow approach. Our aim is to encompass and synergize all facets of a capability, including people, processes, technology, and information, with the option of going into greater detail if needed. Therefore, these decisions should be taken at the capability level, so that they set a precedent for the capability and provide a foundational guide for the subsequent design of the operating model. Taking this kind of holistic approach for a

complete capability will ensure that the different operational dimensions follow the same vision and will be aligned
as components of one system.

Later in this book, we'll explore the ramifications for the
operating model in further detail and offer some practical
guidelines. Nevertheless, within any organization, aligning
the strategic profile of each capability with the overarching
strategic vision is a critical step for all capabilities. When
a capability is identified as a commodity, opting for a standardization profile emerges as a logical and valid strategy.

The differentiation profile as it stands, however, strikes
me as too broad. I prefer to split it into two distinct options—
output differentiation and *cost differentiation*. Output differentiation hinges on distinguishing capabilities by the uniqueness of their outputs, be it services or products, internally
and externally. If a competitive advantage is attainable by
offering an outcome unmatched by competitors, this profile is justified. Externally, it could manifest as unparalleled
product or service quality that ensures customer loyalty.
Internally, it might take the form of superior HR services
that enhance training and talent retention.

Cost differentiation, by contrast, is about structuring
capabilities to reduce costs, contributing to lower-priced
offerings. However, this pathway is not as straightforward
as it might seem. Despite its appeal as an alternative to
standardization, cost differentiation demands deliberate
effort and prioritization. It is most relevant when cost leadership is the overarching strategic choice, as seen in the
case of a deep discounter like Ryanair, the low-cost Irish
airline famous for its aggressive cost-cutting strategies. In
instances where neither output nor cost differentiation are
applicable, standardization often becomes the default strategy. To my mind, standardization should equate to delivering

"good enough quality at a good enough cost," adhering to market standards.

The final profile centers on innovation, which is apt if you envision organizing a capability that yields groundbreaking products or services, with operational costs of secondary concern. Here, the emphasis is on the agility to experiment with novel operating methods and outcomes, positioning flexibility at the forefront of strategic priorities. This strategic profile is tailor-made for scenarios where innovation is the key driver of competitive advantage. These are rare, however, as they most often start as innovative, but evolve into output differentiation or cost differentiation.

Below is a more detailed explanation of each of the four strategic profiles and their impact for the operating-model dimensions. This means that, once we have set a strategic profile for a capability, it provides a great guide for those who need to make decisions on operating-model dimensions related to those capabilities. Diverting from this should be done with caution, and only when good arguments can be found.

Strategic Profiles for Capabilities: Four options

STRATEGIC PROFILE 1: Standardization

Description: This profile gives way to the use of stable, reliable operating models or systems that prioritize efficiency in supporting core processes and managing data.

Explanation: Standardization is the foundation of operational continuity, offering no direct competitive advantage but ensuring "good enough quality at a good enough cost" in alignment with market standards. However, failing to meet market standards might result in a weaker competitive position.

It's the go-to profile when neither differentiation nor innovation is a strategic fit, embodying common sense in cost structures and business practices. Changes are thoroughly tested before being implemented.

Impact on operating-model dimensions

a **Processes:** Emphasis on streamlined, repeatable processes that are scalable and provide consistent results. The organization adopts and conforms to whatever the market standard is. Processes are designed for ease of monitoring and control.

b **People:** Roles are well-defined, with a certain focus on operational excellence and efficiency but in line with what the market standard prescribes. Training focuses on best practices and adherence to procedures.

c **IT Applications and Information:** Utilization of stable and proven technology platforms that support the status quo. Data is managed for reliability and integrity, supporting standardized reporting and decision-making. IT tactic: buy and adopt.

STRATEGIC PROFILE 2: Cost differentiation

Description: Cost differentiation leads to organizing a capability to enable the offering of products or services at a lower cost than competitors. Innovation is focused solely on cost-cutting.

Explanation: Cost differentiation requires targeted efforts and a strategic approach, so an organization needs to work hard to go beyond the market standards when it comes to optimizing for efficiency. It is relevant when an organization's overarching strategy leans towards cost leadership, aiming for cost savings across all aspects of the business.

This approach is crucial for businesses like deep discounters, where cost efficiency is at the core of their value proposition.

In most cases, multiple capabilities will have to be organized this way to lower the cost structure of the organization to a low enough level to offer products or services at a discounted price, as supporting capabilities will generate overhead costs which are eventually added to the cost of goods and services. The concept of lean, a management approach focused on optimizing your operations for efficiency, is related to this.

Impact on operating-model dimensions

a   **Processes**: Lean processes that eliminate waste and reduce costs, with a focus on achieving economies of scale. Process optimization is ongoing to ensure the lowest operational costs.

b   **People**: Efficiency and cost-awareness are valued skills. Training emphasizes cost-control measures, the optimization of workflows, and creating very efficient specialized profiles, not generalists.

c   **IT Applications and Information**: Technology that drives process efficiency and automation to reduce labor costs. Information systems are designed to monitor cost drivers and facilitate cost-effective decision-making. (IT tactic: buy and adapt, build your own.)

STRATEGIC PROFILE 3: Output differentiation
Description: The focus here is on differentiating based on the unique outcomes of a capability, which may include more innovative services or products for internal and external stakeholders. However, the focus here is not on generating groundbreaking ideas: for such situations, Strategic Profile 4 (innovation) is more fitting. Six Sigma, a management app-

roach which focuses on optimizing your operations for quality, is related to the strategic profile of output differentiation.

Explanation: This profile is chosen when a competitive advantage is sought through distinctive outputs that competitors cannot replicate right away, or that responds to a specific market demand. It can relate to offering unique customer experiences or creating internal efficiencies, such as enhanced HR services that contribute to superior training and talent management.

Impact on operating-model dimensions

a　**Processes**: Less rigid processes that can be customized to deliver differentiated services or products. Processes may be adapted frequently to respond to customer feedback and competitive dynamics.

b　**People**: Talent management focuses on creativity and customer-centric skills to deliver unique outputs. Continuous learning is encouraged to adapt to evolving market needs.

c　**IT Applications and Information**: Systems are chosen for their ability to support customization and change at an acceptable rate. Data analytics plays a key role in understanding customer needs and driving product innovation. (IT tactic: buy and adapt, build your own.)

Strategic Profile 4: Innovation
Description: This strategic profile is characterized by a focus on developing capabilities that foster novel products or services, with a greater emphasis on the flexibility and speed of innovation than on the cost of operations.

Explanation: Innovation-driven capabilities are designed for rapid change and responsiveness to new opportunities, often involving trial and experimentation of new operational methods. The cost is secondary to the potential for breakthroughs that could significantly disrupt the market or create entirely new markets.

Impact on operating-model dimensions

a **Processes**: Dynamic and non-linear processes that support rapid development and iteration. The focus is on speed-to-market and the flexibility to pivot as needed.

b **People**: An agile culture is required to promote experimentation, and accepts the risk of failure as a path to innovation. Employees are empowered to think creatively and act quickly.

c **IT Applications and Information**: Advanced, cutting-edge technologies that support fast prototyping and iteration. Information systems are built to handle ambiguity and rapidly changing data inputs, fostering an environment of continuous innovation. (IT tactic: build your own.)

Mapping Porter's strategies to the Strategic Profiles for Capabilities

The table below (figure 4.3) presents a comprehensive mapping that aligns the four strategic profiles with Porter's strategic frameworks, aiding in the decision-making process for capability development. It's important to note that standardization is universally applicable, acting as a solid foundation for any strategic direction. For capabilities that don't yield a competitive advantage or aren't aimed at cost reduction, standardization remains a sensible choice, adhering to industry norms.

One final note here is that standardization should be seen as an eventual goal. In some cases, capabilities may be in an ad hoc state and not yet on par with competitors. While it could be argued that an ad hoc (or below par) state might serve as a temporary strategic profile (particularly for startups), this is often a matter of prioritization. Even in such cases, Standardization probably remains the long-term objective, it's just that the necessary investments to achieve it may not be justified at this stage.

Strategic Profile for Capabilities ▶ Porter's Strategies ▼	No innovation	Limited innovation		High level of innovation
	Standardization	Cost differentiation	Output differentiation	Innovation
Cost leadership	Always relevant	High relevance	Lower relevance	Lower relevance
Differentiation	Always relevant	Lower relevance	High relevance	Possibly relevant
Focus	Always relevant	Lower relevance	High relevance	High relevance

FIGURE 4.3 Mapping Porter's strategies
to Strategic Profiles for Capabilities

When pursuing cost leadership, the cost differentiation profile often takes precedence due to its direct impact on reducing expenses and enhancing competitiveness through price. However, for strategies centered on differentiation or focus, output differentiation and innovation become more relevant, fostering unique product offerings or pioneering new market approaches respectively.

While Porter's models provide strategic direction, they also allow for a mix-and-match approach when necessary. A thorough capability analysis can reveal how combining different strategic profiles may serve overarching business goals. It's this nuanced and tailored application of strategic profiles that empowers organizations to craft an operating model aligned with their unique competitive landscape.

A final reflection on connected capabilities

Now, let's talk about the dependency between capabilities, a critical aspect of strategic implementation. Often, the ability to organize one capability innovatively depends on the flexibility of related, often supportive, capabilities. For example, if rapid shifts in applications used for realizing specific capabilities are necessary, the IT-related capabilities must be adaptable to facilitate this change. Understanding these dependencies is essential for realizing our strategic vision, as was outlined in Use Case 1.

This interdependency also partly explains why capabilities are often duplicated within an organization, particularly in the context of innovation. Typically, most capabilities are intended to operate in a standardized manner, as they don't directly contribute to a competitive advantage. Consequently, the IT capabilities that support most of an organization's functions are optimized for this standardization. However, certain capabilities that were given the strategic profile of innovation might require a distinct approach that necessitates a different kind of IT support, with special processes and roles that allow for fast change and deployment. This need for differentiation can lead to the duplication (or splitting up) of capabilities to meet specific innovative demands effectively.

Indicating strategic profiles on the CapMap

There are various methods to denote the selected strategic profile for each capability. It is advisable to specify this at the most granular level, because sub-capabilities of a broader capability may require different profiles—say, standardization for some, and differentiation or innovation for others. I suggest using distinct icons to signify the strategic profile of each capability. While other methods, such as color coding or shading, can also be effective, icons offer clarity without precluding the use of color for additional layers of information. Although multiple color codes can be applied to a single capability, it can complicate the visual presentation, whereas icons can maintain a clear and unambiguous representation. Figure 4.4 (below) illustrates this.

Preferred option - using icons

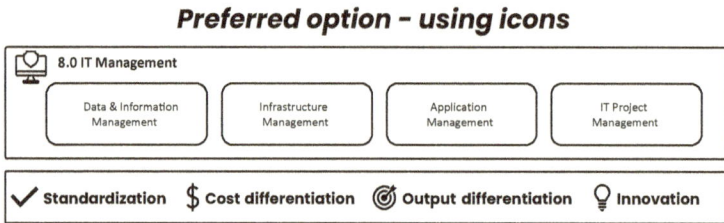

FIGURE 4.4 Illustrating Strategic Profiles for Capabilities on a CapMap

**EXAMPLE CASE: ROYAL BELFOOT—
DECIDING ON STRATEGIC PROFILES FOR CAPABILITIES**

Going back to the Royal BelFoot case, we observe that football clubs embody a unique juxtaposition of sporting and business performances. While sporting achievements often receive more public acclaim, operational and financial successes are equally vital and interdependent. Although Porter's strategic models are not a perfect fit for these kinds of organizations, similar strategic paths can be discerned.

Clubs with limited budgets may parallel a cost leadership strategy, emphasizing cost containment to achieve good results on a limited budget. Others might leverage their resources to pursue differentiation in specific services: customer-facing and internal. For example, in sports operations like scouting and medical services (such as scouting, medical and fitness tracking, performance tracking), clubs might opt for output differentiation or innovation, utilizing advanced analytics and AI to gain a competitive edge.

Transfer management illustrates a hybrid domain: blending sporting and business acumen while applying a different approach could enhance self-sustainability, relying on income from player transfers to balance the budget. In such cases, clubs could innovate in this area, adopting novel strategies for player acquisition and development. Meanwhile, in business operations, clubs can distinguish themselves by offering superior B2B hospitality or digital engagement to fans. However, capabilities such as financial accounting are most often best aligned with a standardization strategy to ensure operational efficiency and compliance. Creative accounting isn't thought of positively.

CBM Use Case 2—Strategic Profiles for Capabilities

Type: Prescriptive

Description: In the strategic profile Use Case of Capability-Based Management, the essence lies in aligning each capability with the organization's overarching strategic vision. This process involves categorizing capabilities according to their potential to contribute to competitive advantage—standardization for essential but non-differentiating functions; cost differentiation where cost efficiency is paramount; output differentiation when distinct value can be offered; and innovation for capabilities that will drive market disruption.

The strategic profile Use Case acts as a compass, guiding the development of capabilities in a way coherent with the organization's strategic priorities, ensuring that investments and resources are optimally allocated to those capabilities when changing them to align with the strategic vision promises the greatest return.

Audience: Multiple stakeholders, e.g., Senior Management (C-suite), Board of Directors, Middle Management.

Main facilitator: External consultant (facilitator) or internal analysts (Strategic Analyst, Enterprise Architect), with input from key stakeholders (Leadership Team, Senior IT Manager, Enterprise Architects).

What main actions are needed? Interviewing the stakeholders, facilitating workshops, defining strategic profiles for the capabilities, and indicating these decisions on the map.

Information captured: A desired strategic profile is assigned to each capability. However, it is crucial to emphasize that since this strategic profile is relative to the market situation, a thorough competitive market analysis is essential.

Information plotted on CapMap: Capabilities on the map are marked with an icon to illustrate the strategic profile assigned.

Preconditions: A Capability Map should be present and accepted by the different parties. Strategic goals/ambitions should be clear and aligned.

4.2.4   USE CASE 3: SWOT Analysis

Of all the analysis models in a strategist's toolkit, the SWOT analysis is arguably the most renowned, but also often criticized for its frequent misuse and oversimplification of reality. However, many scholars and practitioners have stated that there is true value in conducting a SWOT analysis in the strategic process, as long as it is done with care and the gravity of the conclusions derived from it reflect the level of quality of the analysis [25].

Similar to the previous Use Cases, I believe it is beneficial to perform this analysis at a more granular level within the organization as well, time and budget permitting. I contend that the SWOT analysis should be integral to the process of determining strategic profiles for different capabilities, as it helps to reflect on the market position. Taking the SWOT analysis to the capability level enables an organization to evaluate the strengths, weaknesses, opportunities, and threats of specific capabilities, and makes the causes for the considered relative competitive position of the organization more specific or tangible.

While SWOT analysis at the organizational level remains valuable, applying it to individual capabilities offers a deeper understanding of the internal strengths and weaknesses of the organization as it focuses on the internal building blocks—the capabilities. The external factors (namely, opportunities and threats) are determined by examining market conditions, government regulations, and other external influences. By tracing these factors down to the impacted capabilities, we gain a more nuanced understanding of their implications for the organization.

The table below shows some examples of components to consider when conducting a SWOT analysis for capabilities. This should serve only as a guide, as it is ultimately up to the analyst to determine the relevant factors for each capability. Numerous authors have provided extensive insights on conducting SWOT analyses at the organizational level, offering ample reference for those seeking more detailed methods.

Capability SWOT analysis

Strengths
Identify the internal factors that give the capability an advantage compared to others in the market.

- Efficient processes
- Skilled workforce (considering competencies and numbers)
- Advanced technology and tools
- Strong information systems and data management
- Effective leadership and governance

Weaknesses
Identify the internal factors that place the capability at a disadvantage compared to others in the market.

- Inefficient or outdated processes
- Skill gaps or lack of expertise among personnel
- Inadequate or obsolete technology
- Poor information management or data quality issues
- Lack of clear direction or support from leadership

Opportunities
Identify the external factors that the organization can exploit to its advantage for a specific capability.

- Emerging market trends
- Technological advancements
- Changes in regulatory environment
- Partnerships and collaborations
- New customer segments or needs

Threats
Identify the external factors that could cause trouble for a specific capability.

- Competitive pressures
- Rapid technological changes rendering current tools obsolete
- Changes in regulations or compliance requirements
- Shifts in customer preferences or market demand

The example below illustrates the outcome of a SWOT analysis for a specific capability. While this example is specific to the Royal BelFoot Football Club's situation, it can be easily adapted to organizations in other industries. Here, the SWOT analysis was conducted at the Level 1 capability level. As always, it is up to the analyst to determine the most appropriate level of analysis in order to derive the best insights.

Strengths
- Well-trained and customer-focused staff
- Robust CRM (Customer Relationship Management) system
- High customer satisfaction scores
- Strong knowledge base and information management

Weaknesses
- High turnover rates among customer service representatives
- Inconsistent service levels across different channels
- Outdated website and app
- Limited integration between CRM and other systems

Opportunities
- Adoption of AI and chatbots for faster customer and fan service
- Implementing advanced analytics for better customer insights
- Developing self-service portals for customers (fans and B2B partners)

Threats
- Increasing competition with superior customer service offerings
- Rising customer expectations for faster and more personalized service
- Regulatory changes affecting customer data handling
- Economic fluctuations impacting partner and sponsorship budgets

SWOT analysis and the capability structure

While indicating the outcomes of decisions or the status on the CapMap can be valuable for other Use Cases, the SWOT analysis is different. As a descriptive tool, the SWOT analysis collects information and makes judgments, but does not prescribe guiding principles. It serves primarily as a data collection Use Case, facilitating decisions and supporting other analyses and Use Cases.

For this reason, the optimal way to document SWOT findings is in a matrix form. In this format, the first column lists the capabilities, followed by columns for strengths, weaknesses, opportunities, and threats. Analyzing these elements across different capabilities might even reveal patterns or recurring issues, suggesting areas where action may be necessary.

CBM Use Case 3 — SWOT Analysis for Capabilities

Type: Descriptive

Description: The SWOT analysis Use Case in Capability-Based Management focuses on evaluating the strengths, weaknesses, opportunities, and threats associated with each capability. This descriptive analysis provides valuable insights into the internal and external factors affecting each capability. By systematically collecting and evaluating this information, organizations can better understand their capabilities' strategic positions and identify areas requiring attention or improvement.

Audience: Multiple stakeholders, e.g., Senior Management (C-suite), Board of Directors, Middle Management, Strategic Planners.

Main facilitator: External consultants or internal analysts (e.g., Strategic Analyst, Enterprise Architect), with input from key stakeholders (Leadership Team, Senior IT Manager, Enterprise Architects, Business Analysts).

What main actions are needed? Collecting data through market studies, interviews, surveys, and workshops; analyzing data to identify strengths, weaknesses, opportunities, and threats; documenting findings in a SWOT matrix.

Information captured: The SWOT analysis captures detailed information about the strengths, weaknesses, opportunities, and threats related to each capability. This information is crucial for facilitating further strategic decision-making and supporting other analyses and Use Cases.

Information plotted on CapMap: Unlike other Use Cases, the SWOT analysis does not directly plot information on the CapMap. Instead, the findings are documented in a matrix format, listing capabilities and their corresponding strengths, weaknesses, opportunities, and threats.

Preconditions: A capability structure should be present and accepted by the different parties. Strategic goals/ambitions should be clear and aligned to a certain degree.

4.2.5   USE CASE 4:
Operational Resource Mapping

Like the SWOT analysis, Use Case 4—operational resource mapping—is another descriptive Use Case. However, this case specifically focuses on analyzing the current operational landscape of the organization and mapping this information to the capabilities. Each capability's operational dimensions (Process, People, Information, and Technology) reflect resources (broadly defined to include non-tangible elements like processes) that can be mapped to capabilities. Collecting this information is valuable, as it helps trace the relationships between capabilities and operational resources, facilitating further analysis and understanding of impacts when changes occur. (This is particularly relevant for Fit-Gap analysis, as explained in Use Case 5.)

The data we can collect and link includes:

- **IT systems and applications (digital enablers).** This mapping is done primarily from a functional perspective, helping us understand which capabilities are supported by which applications (and identifying interrelated capabilities). While it could be detailed further by linking processes to applications, this added complexity may not be advisable in the early stages. I sometimes refer to this dimension as the "digital enablers." In essence, digital solutions like IT applications enable the organization to execute their operations and create value.

- **Processes**. It's debatable if processes are part of this phase: while it's a valuable component if the goal is to gain a deeper understanding of the core processes within a capability or to assess them in detail, it might also spark unwanted discussion on the scope of the processes. Another reason to include it might be to discover processes that span multiple capabilities, but, again, this analysis can be time-consuming and may complicate the overall overview. I would recommend this only for analyzing at a deeper operational level.

- **Key information objects**. Information is crucial for executing processes. Identifying key information (or data) necessary for proper capability execution helps assess data quality and determine if a capability is at risk of meeting expectations.

- **People roles**. Understanding which roles are essential for the realization of capabilities (and the execution of their processes) is vital. Identifying existing or required roles allows for later analysis of the availability of required competencies, which is crucial for the Fit-Gap analysis.

If you don't have time to thoroughly analyze and map all operational dimensions, focus on mapping the IT application landscape and limiting the scope to those capabilities considered to be in focus for the strategic ambitions. In my experience, this yields the most significant insights for further analysis and helps determine whether your IT landscape (and related IT strategy) supports your organization's strategic vision.

Operational resource mapping and the capability structure
Like the SWOT analysis Use Case, operational research mapping also serves primarily as a descriptive tool. Its

main function is to collect data, facilitating decisions and supporting other analyses and Use Cases. While mapping IT applications on a CapMap is possible, it often results in visual information overload. Therefore, the optimal way to document this data is in a matrix format.

I recommend using different matrices for different operational dimensions. Each matrix should have the first column listing the capabilities, followed by columns for the different IT applications. At each intersection, indicate whether it's a core or supporting application (as illustrated in figure 4.5). This approach further allows for filtering specific capabilities or applications, providing immediate insight into which applications and capabilities are interconnected and would thus be impacted by changes. It also allows us to grasp the extent of issues associated with specific applications. A similar approach can be taken for other operational dimensions.

	IT Application 1	IT Application 2	IT Application 3	IT Application 4
Capability A	C	C	–	–
Capability B	–	–	–	C
Capability C	S	C	–	–

FIGURE 4.5 Mapping IT applications and capabilities

CBM Use Case 4—Operational Resource Mapping

Type: Descriptive

Description: The operational resource mapping Use Case in Capability-Based Management focuses on analyzing the organization's current operational landscape and mapping this information to the capabilities. This descriptive analysis provides valuable insights into how operational dimensions (Process, People, Information, and Technology) are utilized within each capability. By systematically collecting and mapping this information, organizations can better understand the relationships between capabilities and operational resources, facilitating further analysis and supporting strategic decision-making.

Audience: Multiple stakeholders, e.g., Senior Management (C-suite), Board of Directors, Middle Management, IT Managers, Strategic Planners.

Main facilitator: External consultants or internal analysts (e.g., Strategic Analyst, Enterprise Architect), with input from key stakeholders (Leadership Team, Senior IT Manager, Enterprise Architects, Technical Architect, Solution Architect, Process Analyst, Business Analysts).

What main actions are needed? Collecting data through interviews, surveys, and workshops; mapping operational resources (e.g., IT systems, processes, information objects, people roles) to capabilities; documenting findings in a matrix format.

Information captured: Detailed information about the IT systems and applications, processes, key information objects, and people roles associated with each capability. This data is essential for understanding the current operational landscape and identifying potential areas for improvement or realignment through further Use Cases.

Information plotted on CapMap: While it is possible to map IT applications and other resources on the CapMap, this often results in information overload. Therefore, the findings are best documented in a matrix format. Separate matrices for different operational dimensions can be used, with capabilities listed in the first column and corresponding operational resources in subsequent columns, indicating core and supporting relationships.

Preconditions: A capability structure should be present and accepted by the different parties.

4.2.6   USE CASE 5: Fit-Gap Analysis

Use Case 5 is pivotal for strategic decision-making, as it involves a Fit-Gap analysis to assess how well current capabilities are aligned with the strategic vision outlined in earlier Use Cases. This means that Use Cases 1, 2, and 3 are essential prerequisites for this Use Case—after all, without a clear future vision for capabilities, it's unfeasible to accurately gauge the present state and identify the necessary steps to achieve the envisioned future state. In addition, since executing a Fit-Gap analysis for each capability requires an understanding of the current IT landscape of the organization and the current processes, Use Case 4 can also be considered a necessary prerequisite.

Many organizations are accustomed to conducting Fit-Gap analyses at an operational level, often through requirements engineering for improvements of processes or for the development of applications. Applying a similar approach at a strategic level presents its own challenges. First, strategic analysis can be complex and costly, so focusing on capabilities identified as strategically important may be the most prudent approach given time and budget constraints. Ideally, all capabilities would be analyzed to ensure the robustness of any assumptions, but it's always wise to start with those marked for strategic focus.

Second, there is the level of abstraction. On a capability level, we can productively abstract from the operational configuration for certain analyses and discussions in order to avoid loss of focus. However, while it's possible to ascertain whether a capability aligns with the future vision at a higher level, the "confidence level" of the assessment depends on the level of analysis. If we keep it on the capability level, the confidence level is lower; conversely, if we delve deeper into the operational dimensions of that capability, the confidence level of the analysis increases.

Strategic decisions often hinge on a balance of educated assumptions and, where possible, insights from data analysis. When extensive data analysis is not viable due to time or budget constraints, relying on the expertise and informed judgement of management and experts is a viable alternative. Planning poker [26], an agile approach, is an example of a technique that can be mimicked here, enabling stakeholders to rate each capability as underfit (not good enough compared to the goal expectations or strategic profile), fit (everything is in line), or overfit (you have invested heavily in customizing a capability which has received a Standardized strategic profile) in relation to their strategic profiles and objectives. These evaluations are still at a higher, more abstract capability level, resulting in a naturally lower confidence level.

Note that no matter which level you conduct the analysis on (capability, or the underlying operational dimensions), you need to set clear indicators that reflect what is expected. Saying something is fit naturally needs more nuance and a benchmark or bar to compare it with. Defining performance indicators that reflect the levels (underfit, fit, overfit) is an important part of this analysis.

Increasing the depth of analysis therefore enhances confidence. Delving into the operational dimensions is advisable for a granular and more assured analysis, time and budget permitting. As the analysis descends into the operating-model dimensions, the confidence in the findings is increased. This enables a detailed examination of whether the applications and processes align with the predefined goals and strategic profiles of the focused capabilities. (You will find a comprehensive list of investigation topics for applications and information quality for this deeper analysis later in this book.)

Quantity and quality counts

Practitioners have a variety of methods for data collection and analysis at their disposal. In employing these analytical approaches, organizations can gain a multifaceted view of their operations with principally two types of data to consider: *quantitative* and *qualitative*. Quantitative data—i.e., data that is measurable and amenable to statistical methods—is often considered to be more objective, but gathering and analyzing this type of data within organizations can be both challenging and resource-intensive. Below is a more detailed illustration of how to collect quantitative data for the different operating-model dimensions of a capability.

Quantitative data at different operational dimensions

- **Processes**: Consultants often conduct process analysis measuring output and throughput rates, among other metrics, to uncover efficiencies and bottlenecks.

- **People**: Performance metrics such as active hours and engagement rates provide objective data, while competencies might be evaluated through testing, scoring, and external certifications.

- **Information (and Data)**: While aspects like timeliness and data availability can be readily quantified, the accuracy of data often demands subjective evaluation alongside objective measurement.

- **Technology**: Metrics such as system availability and deploy time offer insight into technological robustness; quality attributes described in the book *Software Architecture in Practice* [27] provide a comprehensive framework for evaluation.

Qualitative data, in contrast to quantitative, offers information grounded in observation and description, capturing the subtleties and context that numbers alone may overlook. This form of data is indispensable for a comprehensive analysis, particularly when the intricacies of real-life phenomena are critical.

The notion that qualitative data lacks analytical rigor is a misconception. The objective here is not to uncover a singular "absolute truth," but to identify patterns that can inform sound decision-making. For this reason, it is prudent to incorporate qualitative data collection into the strategic process. While quantitative data provides specificity, qualitative data contributes context and depth, painting a more holistic picture that is vital for nuanced insights and informed strategic choices. Below are more details of how qualitative information or data can be captured.

Qualitative data: collection techniques

- **Observation**: Observing how individuals work and interact in their teams can uncover the reality of how processes are executed and not just how they should be. It can also provide insights into cultural dynamics and team atmospheres that quantitative data may not reveal. These observations, while not quantifiable, are crucial in understanding the qualitative aspects of work execution.

- **Interviews**: One of the most prevalent techniques in qualitative data collection is the interview, either one-on-one or in focus groups, in which the aim is to discern patterns. Typically, interview transcripts are *coded*—an analytical method where statements are categorized (with codes) to highlight recurring themes, such as comments on an IT system's reliability. Such data then enables pattern recognition. For a more in-depth exploration of this analytical method, Saldaña [28] is a noted reference; although it's a more academic treatment of the subject, the techniques it covers are also of great value in a business environment. (An illustrative example and potential codes will be provided later.)

- **Surveys**: Surveys are versatile tools for eliciting information, capable of accommodating open-ended questions as well as scaled responses, typically ranging from 1 to 7, facilitating subsequent data analysis. Surveys are particularly effective in confirming previously identified patterns and observations, such as those obtained from interviews.

- **Workshops**: Workshops are collaborative sessions designed to jointly uncover new insights, which can also be applied if you're unsure what you're looking for yet but want to work towards a consensus with the participants. These sessions require meticulous preparation and facilitation skills to guide participants toward a shared understanding or consensus.

Each qualitative data collection method offers distinct advantages and contributes to a richer understanding of organizational dynamics. The choice of method should align with the specific objectives of your analysis and the depth of insight required.

The final aim of collecting and analyzing this data—quantitative or qualitative—is to make a judgement call on the current situation compared to the envisioned or desired future state. This judgment is expressed through a fit-value assessment, categorizing capabilities and their operational dimensions as underfit, fit, or overfit (which we'll cover in more detail later on). Figure 4.6 provides an illustration of the increased confidence vote, related to the type of data collected and analyzed.

Confidence level

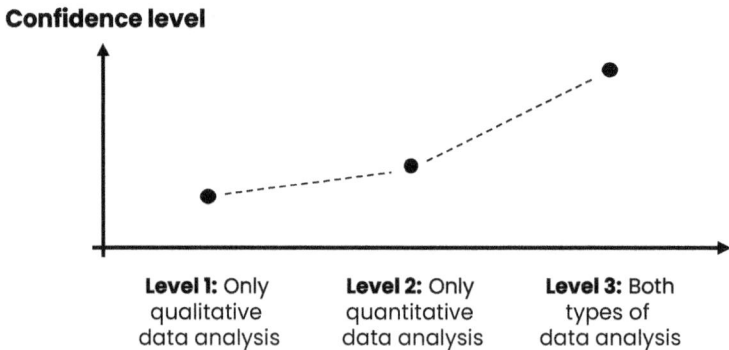

Level 1: Only	**Level 2:** Only	**Level 3:** Both
qualitative	quantitative	types of
data analysis	data analysis	data analysis

FIGURE 4.6 The more profound the analysis,
the higher the confidence level

The scope and depth of your analysis will invariably be influenced by time and budget constraints. It is unrealistic to expect comprehensive quantitative data across all dimensions of every capability. In practice, initiating the analysis with interviews and surveys often yields substantial insights.

Critical to this approach is the careful selection of interview participants. While existing reports and documentation serve as useful references when time is short, a multifaceted approach that combines various techniques can substantially enhance the reliability of a Fit-Gap analysis.

However, in the realm of strategic decision-making, people must navigate the delicate balance between the need for certainty and the urgency of action. Aiming for absolute certainty may lead to decision paralysis, stifling progress. It is essential, then, to temper the quest for comprehensive data with pragmatic decision-making, ensuring that a quest for perfect information does not hinder timely and decisive action.

Possible areas of interest for data collection

The table below outlines a range of potential properties that analysts might consider when assessing the state of IT systems and solutions associated with a particular capability, including evaluating the quality of information related to the application under investigation. Note that this list is intended as a starting point and source of inspiration—it is the responsibility of the analyst to determine the specific aspects to investigate, the methods of measurement and scoring, and the weighting of these factors in the final calculation of a fit-value.

PROPERTY NAME	VALUE	QUALITY TYPE
End-of-life	Date	N/A
Current scalability	Value	Technical quality
Assessed scalability	Value	Technical quality
Assessed performance	Value	Technical quality
Assessed security level	Value	Technical quality
Assessed stability	Value	Technical quality
Estimated value for money	Value	Cost
Current total cost per year	Number	Cost
Tolerated total cost per year	Number	Cost
TIME* value	Value	N/A
Business criticality**	Value	N/A
Efficiency support	Value	Business fit
Functional coverage	Value	Business fit
Correctness	Value	Business fit
Future potential	Value	Business fit
Completeness	Value	Information quality
Correctness	Value	Information quality
Availability	Value	Information quality
Timeliness	Value	Information quality

* The TIME [46] value is given to an IT system or application, after analysis. It carries a judgment on the application and explicates the plans for the application.

We either Tolerate, Invest (in), Eliminate, or Migrate the application.

** There are multiple scaling models, but I would suggest going from **Critical** (if the application goes down, all operations related to the application stop) to **Medium** (a short downtime is acceptable) to **Low** (there are manual alternatives, even a longer downtime of a few days is not the worst case). You can check other models for inspiration, e.g., Doval [29].

Visualizing the data on the CapMap

After the data collection and analysis phase is complete, the synthesized results can be mapped onto the CapMap. Note that not all collected data can be directly displayed on the CapMap, due to its complexity; therefore, a supplementary matrix should be maintained to house the detailed values for each investigated capability and the different elements that reflect the operational dimensions. However, for strategic decision-making purposes, data must be consolidated into a more abstract form suitable for representation on the CapMap.

Typically, three types of information are crucial for each capability:

- **Confidence level/vote**: This metric indicates how much trust we have in the data and subsequent analysis.

- **Fit-value for each operating-model dimension**: Data from each dimension should be aggregated into one value that reflects the overall state of that particular dimension for a specific capability.

- **Overall fit-value for the capability**: The fit-values from various dimensions must be combined into one metric that captures the holistic fitness of the capability.

Confidence level reflects robustness

The confidence level is a nuanced addition that reflects the robustness of the underlying analysis. The analyst can decide the extent of information displayed on the CapMap and whether or not to include it, omitting the confidence level if it does not serve the strategic purpose. I advocate for its inclusion, as it provides context to the displayed values. A low confidence level, especially when the ensuing decisions carry significant weight, might necessitate further investigation to bolster certainty before committing to a course of action. This metric can be visualized on the CapMap with a distinct letter code for each capability, ranging from Level 1 (L1) to Level 2 (L2) to Level 3 (L3), in line with the values presented in figure 4.6 above.

Fit-value for the capability

On the CapMap, the overall fitness of each capability is represented by a single traffic-light indicator in the form of an arrow. This indicator synthesizes the collective assessments of all operational dimensions—Processes, People, Information, and Applications/Technology—into one comprehensive visual cue.

A *red*, upward-pointing arrow indicates that the capability is generally significantly underfit, suggesting a significant need for enhancement (or upgrade) to meet strategic goals. The *yellow* arrow, pointing to the right, indicates that the capability is underfit, but that it is acceptable and actions for improvement should be considered a lower priority. A *green* arrow pointing to the right signifies that the capability is well-aligned with strategic requirements and is performing effectively. A *blue*, downward-pointing arrow shows that the capability is overfit, indicating potential overinvestment or excessive capability beyond what is strategically necessary, and thus demanding a downgrade.

This simplified traffic-light system provides a clear and immediate overview for decision-makers, facilitating swift and informed strategic evaluations and adjustments. The same can be done for the underlying operational dimensions, where the same color coding is applied. Each of the four blocks represents an operational dimension: Processes, People, Information, and Applications/Technology. (It is important to always use the same sequence to avoid confusion.) The letter in the colored boxes reflects the color itself, to increase readability (**R**ed, **Y**ellow, **G**reen, **B**lue).

By incorporating this information, the CapMap becomes an effective tool for informing strategic choices, ensuring that decisions are made with an appropriate degree of confidence in the supporting data. Figure 4.7 shows how this can be done in practice.

Enriching the CapMap with Fit-Gap Analysis info

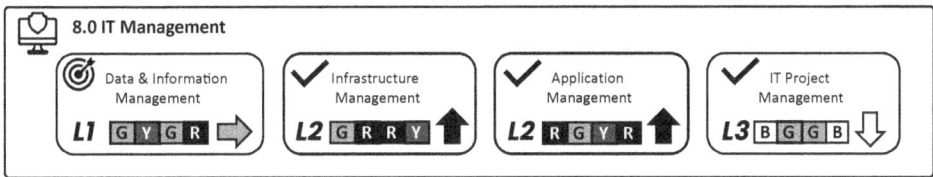

FIGURE 4.7 Indicating the outcome of the Fit-Gap analysis on the CapMap

Analysis on the CapMap
This Use Case illustrates a crucial initial descriptive phase in our capability analysis. It doesn't prescribe immediate actions, but rather lays out a clear depiction of each capability's current fitness relative to strategic objectives. By illustrating the fitness-values, this approach facilitates structured investigation and meaningful dialogue, providing a strategic canvas to guide investment decisions. The insights reveal which capabilities are performing well (compared to previously expressed expectations) and which require enhancement to align with their strategic importance and assigned profile. This analysis is instrumental in identifying where to channel resources effectively in order to optimize organizational performance.

The subsequent steps involve quantifying the effort needed to elevate each capability through targeted programs and projects. Business cases are then developed for these initiatives, taking the priorities and budget constraints into account. This feeds into the portfolio management process, leading to a well-defined roadmap for implementing change. Such a structured approach ensures that investments are made where they can generate the most value, steering the organization towards its strategic goals.

A similar Use Case can be imagined. Rather than using the CapMap for strategic analysis, it can also be used for operational monitoring, reflecting the current performance compared to predefined targets for specific PIs. In such cases, the assessment value will be underperforming, on track, or overperforming.

CBM Use Case 5—Fit-Gap Analysis

Type: Descriptive

Description: The Fit-Gap analysis serves as a crucial evaluative step within Capability-Based Management, scrutinizing each capability across four key organizational dimensions: Process, People, Information, and Applications/Technology. It methodically identifies discrepancies between the current operational state and the strategic objectives.

This analysis illuminates areas of overinvestment and pinpoints where enhancements are necessary, guiding decision-makers in aligning capabilities with the strategic importance attributed to them. The ultimate aim is to ensure that each capability is aptly designed and resourced to propel the organization towards its defined goals and ambitions.

Audience: Multiple stakeholders, e.g., Senior Management (C-suite), Board of Directors, Middle Management.

Main facilitator: External consultant (facilitator) or internal analysts (e.g., Strategic Analyst, Enterprise Architect), with input from key stakeholders (for example, Leadership Team, Senior IT Manager, Enterprise Architects, Technical Architect, Solution Architect, Process Analyst, Business Analysts).

What main actions are needed? Multiple actions to collect and analyze data, such as interviewing the stakeholders, facilitating workshops, surveys, conducting process analysis. The results are weighted and indicated on the CapMap.

Information captured: Three types of "status" can be assigned to the capabilities. The first indicates the depth of the analysis and consequent confidence level. The second provides a judgment value related to the fitness of each organizational dimension compared to the strategic vision. The last provides a rolled-up value, consolidating the four fitness values of the operational dimensions for a capability into one overall fitness value.

Information plotted on CapMap: Capabilities are assigned an icon to illustrate the confidence level of the analysis. They are also assigned a color indicator reflecting the fitness value of each operational dimension, and one overall color indicator reflecting that of the entire capability.

Preconditions: A capability structure and map should be present and accepted by the different parties. Strategic goals/ambitions should be clear and aligned. Use Cases 1, 2, 3, and 4 should have been executed previously, as they provide the benchmark future vision and necessary understanding of the related resources on which the Fit-Gap analysis can be based.

4.2.7   USE CASE 6: Outsourcing

Outsourcing is widely recognized in the business world as a strategic management tool—a means to reduce costs, create competitive advantages, and enhance organizational performance [30]. One company (the client) contracts another (the service provider) to manage and execute a specific business function (or organize a capability). This transfer, governed by a contractual agreement, details the services provided and associated fees, committing the client to procuring these services for the duration of the contract. As outsourcing becomes more global—and new digital solutions enable an easier setup—its scope has expanded to encompass more business functions and capabilities than ever before [31].

There are multiple reasons for outsourcing: cost savings (achieving lower costs than in-house), quality enhancements (achieving higher standards than is possible internally), addressing current barriers, organizing a capability, or the need for rapid development where building an internal capability is too costly. Broadly, it can take various forms, from straightforward service contracting to more complex joint ventures, each presenting unique risks and benefits. The analysis for outsourcing is multifaceted, ranging from outsourcing entire capabilities (where another party organizes a capability according to specified criteria) to outsourcing parts of a capability. Although often not considered as outsourcing, decisions such as hiring temporary staff, leasing machinery, or using external applications are effectively a form of the outsourcing dimensions of the operating model, and their effects should thus be analyzed in a fitting manner. (This book primarily focuses on outsourcing at the capability level, as delving into the operational dimensions of outsourcing would require too much further explication for our purposes.)

In determining the suitability of outsourcing, first define through the application of the previous Use Cases what is expected of a capability. The next steps involve evaluating potential partners to manage and execute the capability, and assessing whether the associated risks, such as vendor lock-in or loss of confidentiality and intellectual property, are either acceptable or outweigh the benefits.

While this book does not intend to delve deeply into each facet of outsourcing, it is crucial to consider the following considerations, based on the expectations established through earlier Use Cases, and to develop scenarios for comparison:

- Can we organize the capability internally to meet the strategic expectations outlined?

- If so, what would the transformation costs be to achieve the desired state?

- What are the operational costs of maintaining this state, and what outcomes (quality, output levels) can we expect?

- What are the risks and benefits of internal management versus outsourcing?

- Which outsourcing model best aligns with our needs, and do the benefits justify the risks?

A typical example of outsourcing is that of the "IT Infrastructure Management" capability covered later in this book.

Indicating outsourcing on the CapMap

Strategic decision-making involves clear choices, including which options to explicitly forego. After thorough analysis, both the most relevant candidates for outsourcing and the effective final decisions can be visually represented on the Capability Map using a letter-based code. I opt for this visualization method as it allows integration with other layers of information from previous Use Cases. In the descriptive form, we can present the capabilities marked for potential outsourcing (whether you decide to mark this as outsourcing candidate, with or without specification of the type of outsourcing, is up to the analysts). This information can then be used to discuss with senior management whether the management team wants to move forward with the outsourcing of specific capabilities. When decisions are made, this can also be plotted on the CapMap as a guiding principle for the rest of the organization.

A last remark is on the Fit-Gap analysis, which even capabilities managed via outsourcing require. The main caveat here is that data collection may be more challenging than in-house, which represents another risk. Figure 4.8 illustrates the visual notation on the CapMap used when a capability is (deemed to be) outsourced, marked by an "O." In this example, we do not include the type of outsourcing in the visual representation.

Indicating outsourcing

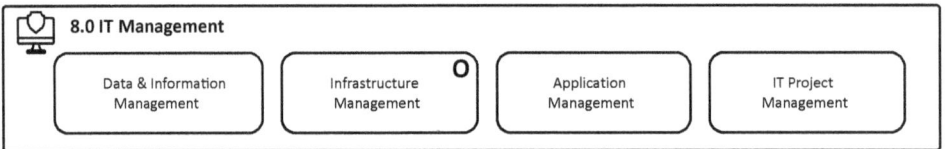

8.0 IT Management

| Data & Information Management | Infrastructure Management | Application Management | IT Project Management |

FIGURE 4.8 Indicating outsourcing decisions on a CapMap in combination with other information

In this specific example, it was decided that the capability of Infrastructure Management should be organized in a standardized manner and outsourced. This reflects a common strategic decision in practice. Managing IT infrastructure requires specialized expertise, and, in most cases, is impractical to fully manage in-house.

The decision to outsource is based on financial considerations and also on risk management. Cybersecurity practices, a crucial aspect of IT infrastructure management, must be continually updated. Outsourcing to specialized providers who excel in this area reduces risk and enhances security. Additionally, this approach allows organizations to focus on their core competencies while leveraging external expertise for complex, non-core functions.

CBM Use Case 6—Outsourcing

Type: Descriptive and Prescriptive

Description: This Use Case focuses on evaluating and deciding the outsourcing of specific capabilities within an organization, a strategic approach to manage specific functions in the most relevant way. It involves analyzing each capability to determine if outsourcing can achieve cost savings, enhance service quality, or address resource constraints. The decision to outsource is based on a comprehensive assessment of capability alignment with strategic goals, considering operational needs and potential risks such as vendor lock-in and loss of control over sensitive information.

Audience: Senior Management (C-suite), Board of Directors, Strategic Planners.

Main facilitator: External consultants or internal analysts (e.g., Strategic Analyst, Enterprise Architect), with substantial input from operational and strategic stakeholders (e.g., Leadership Team, Senior IT Manager).

What main actions are needed? Decisions on outsourcing require rigorous evaluation, including cost-benefit analysis, risk assessment, and alignment checks with strategic objectives. Actions may include conducting interviews, facilitating decision workshops, and leveraging analytical tools to project outcomes and impacts of outsourcing.

Information captured: Key information includes potential cost savings, quality improvements, strategic alignment, and risk profiles for each considered capability. Additionally, scenarios comparing in-house management versus outsourcing options are developed to guide decision-making. All of this should lead to a decision, which can then be plotted on the CapMap.

Information plotted on CapMap: Capabilities considered for outsourcing are marked with an "O" to indicate their status. This helps visualize the parts of the organization's operations managed externally, aligning with strategic decisions about capability sourcing.

Preconditions: A clear and accepted Capability Map is crucial, alongside well-defined strategic goals and a preliminary analysis of existing capabilities (as facilitated by previous Use Cases) to establish a baseline for decision-making.

4.2.8   USE CASE 7: Capability Integration and Standardization Profiles (CISPS)

Up to this point, all of the analysis performed assumes that each capability exists only once. In reality, however, capabilities are often duplicated across multiple locations, subsidiaries, and so on. This means that the analysis and decisions need to be adapted accordingly.

For example, imagine a production company with divisions in the U.S. and Mexico, each with its own production plant. In this case, we would have to decide whether a decision for a specific capability applies to both, or if distinct decisions should be made for each. This adds a layer of complexity to our analysis and decision-making processes. Reflecting on the previous Use Cases, we must determine the appropriate level of analysis and decision-making for each case.

A small caveat here regarding the term "duplication," which is not entirely correct. Each implementation of that specific capability will still require an operational configuration that fits either the U.S.-specific or Mexico-specific context. But, for the sake of simplicity, when two capabilities serve more or less the same scope (e.g., Inbound Logistics in the U.S. factory and Inbound Logistics in the Mexican factory), we will label this as two instances of the same capability.

Additionally, when multiple instances of the same capability exist within one organization, we must consider how to integrate or standardize them. This is crucial for managing multiple locations and finding synergies, ensuring that we maximize efficiency as a group organization. For example, we need to decide which capabilities to organize centrally as shared services (e.g., a capability is organized in the U.S. and the Mexican subsidiary makes use of it), and which to manage locally (a capability that is organized in both the U.S. and the Mexican subsidiary). This raises further questions about the optimal organizational structure.

This Use Case was initially inspired by the works of Jeanne W. Ross, Peter Weill and David C. Robertson, as described in their book *Enterprise Architecture as Strategy* [32], and other research conducted at the MIT Center for Information Systems Research that was led for several years by Prof. Dr. Ross. The authors identify four operating models that organizations can adopt based on the level of integration and standardization of their processes. Integration and standardization are two critical dimensions used to determine the most suitable operating model for an organization which help align business processes and IT infrastructure with the organization's strategy.

Integration and Standardization (after Ross, Weill, Robertson)

Integration refers to the degree to which different business units or processes within an organization must share and access common data, reflecting how much the successful execution of processes in one area depends on another (either operationally or for reporting purposes). High integration indicates that various parts of the organization rely on the same information, necessitating seamless data flow and communication across different units. The advantages of high integration include the ability to offer a consistent customer experience across different locations, as shared data ensures uniformity in interactions.

However, high integration also presents challenges, such as increased costs and time for different parties to agree on an integration format. Additionally, the higher coupling effect between different organizational parts can create dependencies that may slow down operations—e.g., if one subsidiary relies on data from another that is not easily available.

Standardization refers to how uniform the business processes and procedures are across an organization, essentially capturing how advantageous it is to apply the same way of working in various contexts. High standardization means there is a consistent method for performing tasks and processes across different units, driving efficiencies and uniformity in operations. Standardization ensures best practices are followed, making processes predictable and repeatable. Other benefits include increased efficiency through the adoption of such best practices, greater predictability, and the ability to compare and benchmark performance across different subsidiaries.

However, there are downsides to standardization as well, such as the potential loss of local advantages (given that the subsidiary is not catering to specific local needs), and the possibility of resistance or high costs associated with one-size-fits-all solutions.

Despite its value, the model above raises two main concerns. First, while the authors advocate making strategic decisions at a company-wide level (a fundamentally sound approach), Ross's framework, though highly effective at the macro level—where decisions about the overall operating model are made, including the degree of business process standardization and the level of data integration across the organization—does fall short in detailing how these strategic choices are implemented at more granular levels. These limitations are akin to those in Porter's strategies, which tend to overlook the need for flexibility at the finer levels of organizational structure. In my view, these strategic decisions should be made at the more granular capability level, since not all capabilities within an organization should be treated uniformly. (Illustrations of this point follow later in this book.)

Second, the model's broad focus at the higher level ignores a potentially critical fifth option—the shared or central service model. This is particularly relevant at the capability level, where a capability such as Branding (within the Marketing function) could be centrally managed by one subsidiary or the HQ, and then provided as a service to other local subsidiaries. While this omission is understandable given that Ross's model targets a higher level of decision-making, and it would make no sense to use a centralized model as the primary template for the entire organization, the central service model offers a practical and effective strategy that aligns well with the diverse needs of modern organizations.

Below, I have expanded the original four operating model choices into five Capability Integration and Standardization Profiles (CISPs). Each provides a distinct set of directives for configuring the operating-model dimensions of a capability instance, in order to provide a more nuanced approach to strategic decision-making at the capability level.

Capability Integration and Standardization Profiles (CISPs)

Diversification (low integration, low standardization): Capability instances operate independently from each other with unique processes and minimal data-sharing. HR payroll is an example: it's often very different in each country, so might need a diverse approach.

Coordination (high integration, low standardization): Capability instances share data, but develop and maintain different and localized processes. An example is a financial capability where different instances share customer data via a centralized system, but have distinct localized procedures.

Replication (low integration, high standardization): Business units have uniform processes but operate independently with minimal data-sharing. An example is a retail chain where each store follows the same operational procedures (processes) in their logistics capabilities, but function independently.

Unification (high integration, high standardization): Capability instances share data and follow uniform and centrally designed processes. For example, a global manufacturing company has standardized production processes to be deployed in all locations (capability instances). These processes make use of integrated supply chain data.

Centralization (full integration, complete standardization): The capability instances are centrally rather than locally organized. Subsidiaries outsource this capability to HQ or another subsidiary. The central service could also be outsourced.

CISP on the CapMap

Figure 4.9 demonstrates how Capability Integration and Standardization Profiles (CISPs) are depicted on a CapMap. In this example, the capability "Infrastructure Management" has been assigned a "centralization" CISP. This means that all subsidiaries are served by a single instance—potentially the HQ, another subsidiary, or even an external party, as indicated by the "O" in the top right corner of the capability's symbol on the CapMap.

The capabilities "Data Information Management" and "Application Management" have been designated with a "unification" CISP (high integration, high standardization), suggesting that they should be uniformly organized across different subsidiaries and that related data should be consolidated, likely via a central platform. This reflects a commitment to implementing best practices uniformly across the organization.

Note that these capabilities have different strategic profiles (SPs, as defined in Use Case 2). For "Data Information Management," the SP of output differentiation implies that adhering to best practices offers a competitive advantage, suggesting that the organization's standardized internal processes are superior to competitors. In contrast, "Application Management" aims for industry-standard practices used throughout the organization. Another example, not depicted in this figure, involves deep discounters or fast-food chains that typically implement highly (internally) standardized capabilities across all subsidiaries (unification CISP), but their SP for these capabilities is often aligned with cost differentiation. This strategic approach highlights their focus on efficiency and cost control to maintain competitive pricing, compared to others in the market.

Lastly, the figure shows the capability "IT Project Management" with a CISP of replication and an SP of standardization. This suggests a need for integrated data across subsidiaries while allowing for localized process adaptations, aligning with local market standards. This nuanced approach to CISP and SP assignment illustrates the complex considerations involved in organizational strategy implementation.

Indicating Capability Integration & Standardization Profile choices

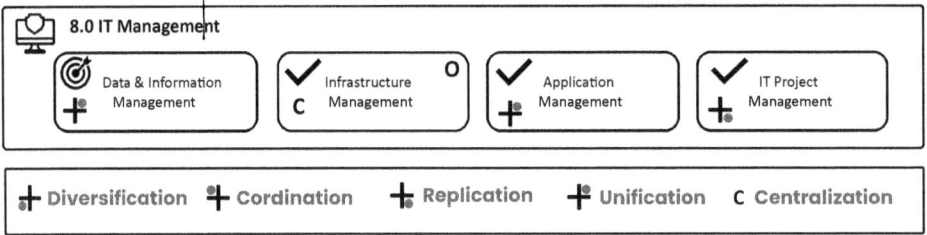

FIGURE 4.9 Indicating Capability Integration and Standardization Profiles (CISPs) on a CapMap

One size fits all?

It is crucial to recognize that these CISP decisions can either be uniform across all instances of a specific capability (as in the previous example), or tailored to individual instances. For example, the HR capability for Recruitment might be assigned a single profile, such as coordination, across all subsidiaries. In this situation, while the data is centralized and subsidiaries utilize a central tool, it's possible to customize the tool to reflect local processes.

Conversely, it may be decided that only specific subsidiaries will adopt the coordination profile, whereas smaller subsidiaries might have the capability organized in a centralized manner by HQ for this specific capability. This demonstrates that decisions do not necessarily have to be applied uniformly to all instances of a capability. It should be noted that conducting the requisite analysis to support these decisions demands considerable effort, and different scenarios must be carefully evaluated against one another.

Finally... on CISP

When comparing CISP to the strategic profile Use Case, it could be argued that assigning a strategic profile reflects an external perspective of the organization, as it entails evaluating the market to determine where the organization can excel by differentiating/innovating and where it is best to stick to market standards. Conversely, decisions regarding the CISP indicate a more internal focus, aimed at identifying the most effective ways to organize a capability across multiple locations. This includes the roll-out of best practices, the exploration of synergies, and similar internal optimizations.

This contrast between external and internal focuses is illustrated in figures 4.10 and 4.11 below.

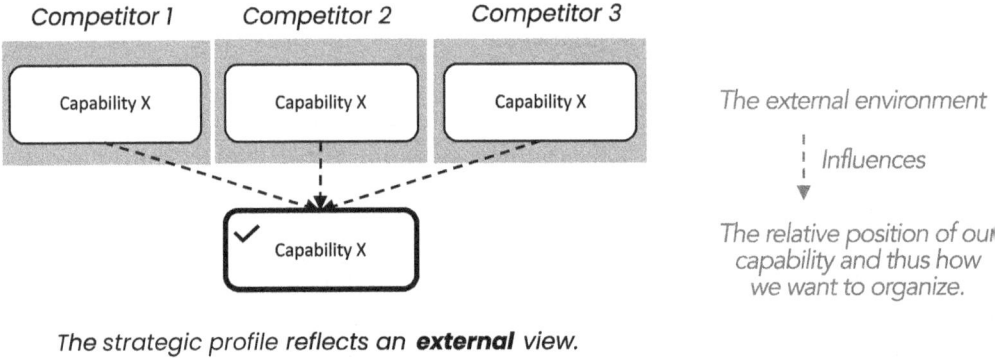

The strategic profile reflects an **external** view.

FIGURE 4.10 Strategic profiles—an external view

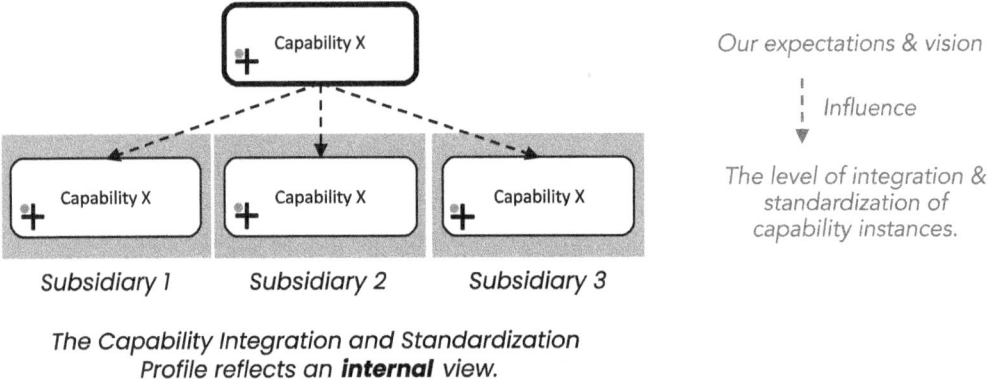

The Capability Integration and Standardization Profile reflects an **internal** view.

FIGURE 4.11 Capability Integration and Standardization Profiles (CISPS)—an internal view

However, there is a notable connection between CISP and the strategic profile's Use Case, particularly concerning the localization of decision-making. Instead of applying a uniform strategic profile across the entire group, consider whether a specific capability's strategic profile should be assessed and assigned based on local needs. In some markets, a differentiating strategy for particular capabilities might provide a competitive advantage, while in others conforming to local standards may be more appropriate. Therefore, it is advisable to evaluate whether to adopt a company-wide strategic profile for a capability, or to customize it according to the specific realities of each local market.

Figure 4.12 illustrates this additional layer of complexity in an organization with multiple locations or subsidiaries, which results in multiple instances of several capabilities. As for Use Case 2 (Strategic Profiles for Capabilities), benchmarking with the market and competitors to decide which SP fits the capabilities can be challenging due to a lack of data. In such cases, strategic analysis often relies on best-effort assumptions, as decisions still need to be made.

A final note concerns the CapMap of such organizations. When dealing with multiple subsidiaries, it is advisable to create a CapMap for each subsidiary and one group view. This allows for analyzing subsidiaries at the appropriate level and clearly shows the decisions made for the group and individual subsidiaries, thus promoting clarity and avoiding confusion.

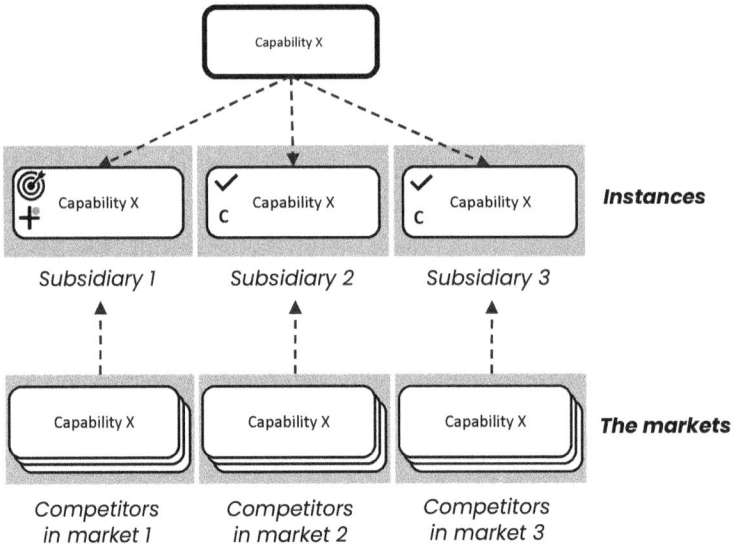

Combining the **Strategic Profile** (internal view) and **Capability Integration and Standardization Profile** (external view) to reflect local market demands.

FIGURE 4.12 Combining Strategic and Capability Integration and Standardization Profiles—a challenging but necessary analysis

CBM Use Case 7—Capability Integration and Standardization Profiles (CISPS)

Type: Prescriptive

Description: This Use Case focuses on the strategic alignment of capabilities across an organization by defining how they should be integrated and standardized. It assesses each capability to determine the most effective organizational structure, to optimize performance and maintain consistency across different entities. The decision-making process considers the operational realities and strategic importance of each capability, aiming to enhance overall organizational efficiency and effectiveness.

Audience: Senior Management (C-suite), Board of Directors, Strategic Planners, Operational Managers.

Main facilitator: Internal analysts (e.g., Enterprise Architect, Strategic Analyst) and operational managers, with input from key stakeholders across the organization (e.g., Department Heads, Managers, Process Owners).

What main actions are needed? The process involves detailed analysis of current capability configurations, workshops to discuss potential integration and standardization, and assessments of operational impact. The findings are used to decide the appropriate CISP for each capability.

Information captured: Data collected includes current operational setups, performance metrics, and stakeholder feedback on each capability. These elements are evaluated to define the optimal integration and standardization level for each capability.

Information plotted on CapMap: Each capability on the CapMap is assigned an indicator for its assigned CISP, representing "diversification," "coordination," "replication," "unification," or "centralization," respectively. This visual representation helps stakeholders quickly understand the strategic layout of capabilities across the organization. It is possible and even advisable to have multiple CapMaps in case of multiple subsidiaries.

Preconditions: An up-to-date and mutually agreed-upon Capability Map is essential, alongside clearly articulated strategic objectives. Prior Use Cases providing insights into the capabilities' current states and strategic importance must have been completed to inform these decisions.

4.2.9   USE CASE 8: Accountability and Responsibility Assignment

In different governance and management frameworks, the RACI chart plays a crucial role. RACI—which stands for (R)esponsible, (A)ccountable, (C)onsulted, and (I)nformed— helps organizations identify the roles or individuals (stakeholders) who are responsible, accountable, consulted with, or informed during/after the execution of a task or work package. In some models, an "S" is added for Supporting roles. A notable example is the COBIT framework [33], where management and governance practices are linked to specified roles in a matrix format, indicating the RACI value for each role versus each practice. (Similarly, in the context of CBM, it is valuable to map out the accountable roles or individuals first; while identifying the responsible parties is also important, it becomes more relevant during the operational assessment phase.)

Responsible refers to the individuals or groups who actually manage and execute a capability—i.e., those who carry out the activities and ensure the capability functions effectively. There can be multiple responsible parties for a given capability, as several individuals or teams may contribute to its operation.

Accountable, on the other hand, designates the individual who ultimately owns the capability and is answerable for its performance. This person has the authority to make decisions regarding the capability and is held accountable for its success or failure. There is typically only one accountable person for each capability, so as to ensure clear ownership and avoid confusion.

In the context of capabilities, it does not seem relevant to identify the C, S, or I roles.

Roles versus names

I would argue that this Use Case should be executed as soon as possible, preferably with specific names rather than just roles, before conducting any other Use Cases. The rationale is that those deemed accountable for a capability are also the ones empowered to make decisions related to them if senior management delegates such authority. In other words, these individuals might need to collaborate on important decisions, such as selecting a strategic profile for a capability or contributing to the gap analysis.

Roles are better practice, as they are more sustainable— i.e., when a role is transferred to a different person, the model won't have to be updated. However, I often prefer names over roles, because they are more concrete, and we need to maintain the model anyway. Although valuable, this Use Case was not initially prioritized as Use Case 1, because the first cases can be conducted with senior management alone if necessary. The ultimate accountable person is often part of the senior management team. I'd argue that it is always wise to execute it as soon as possible.

There are several significant benefits to identifying accountable individuals or roles early on. First, it ensures that all capabilities are covered, with clear accountability assigned. It might seem trivial but, in practice, accountability over capabilities is sometimes avoided (with no one willing to accept it) or contested (with multiple individuals vying for it). Second, identifying accountable individuals helps others in the organization know who to approach for decisions and information related to specific capabilities. This clarity fosters better communication and more efficient decision-making in the organization.

Indicating accountability on the CapMap

There are two valuable ways to display this information on a map or structure. The first is to use a chart, in which the first column lists the different capabilities and the subsequent columns represent the names or roles associated with each capability; at the intersections, you indicate the RA status (see figure 4.13). Naturally, if you are only indicating one accountable person for each capability, you can use a single column and fill in the names at the intersections.

	Name/Role 1	Name/Role 2	Name/Role 3	Name/Role 4
Capability A	A	–	–	–
Capability B	–	A	–	–
Capability C	–	A	–	–

FIGURE 4.13 Indicating accountable roles or
people for capabilities in a matrix structure

The second method is to map out the names directly on the CapMap, as in figure 4.14. In my experience, this approach is highly effective for initiating conversations and for providing guidance to the rest of the organization on basic governance practices.

Indicating accountable/responsible people

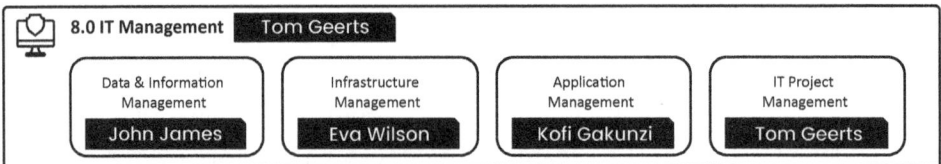

FIGURE 4.14 Indicating accountable
people for capabilities on the CapMap

CBM Use Case 8—Accountability and Responsibility Assignment

Type: Descriptive and Prescriptive

Description: This Use Case focuses on assigning and mapping accountability and (possibly) responsibility for each capability within the organization. The objective is to clearly identify who is responsible for executing each capability and who is accountable for overall performance. This clarity ensures that all capabilities are managed effectively, supporting strategic decision-making and implementation by delineating clear lines of responsibility and accountability.

Audience: Senior Management (C-suite), Board of Directors, Middle Management, Strategic Planners.

Main facilitator: Internal analysts (e.g., Strategic Analyst, Enterprise Architect), with input from key stakeholders (Leadership Team, Senior IT Manager, Department Heads).

What main actions are needed? The process involves identifying the responsible and accountable individuals or roles for each capability, conducting interviews and workshops to validate these assignments, and documenting the findings in a chart or directly on the CapMap.

Information captured: Detailed information about the roles and individuals responsible for and accountable for each capability. This data is crucial for establishing clear governance structures and facilitating effective communication and decision-making within the organization.

Information plotted on CapMap: Capabilities on the CapMap are marked with the names or roles of the accountable individuals. If using a chart, the first column lists the capabilities and subsequent columns list the names or roles, with intersections indicating the RA status.

Preconditions: An established and accepted Capability Map or structure, along with clearly defined strategic goals. Initial Use Cases should have provided a foundational understanding of the capabilities and their strategic importance to inform the accountability and responsibility assignments.

CHAPTER 5

SPECIFIC SCENARIOS
CBM in the Real World:
Guidelines for Navigating
Specific Challenges

"If you don't know where you want to go,
then it doesn't matter what road you take."
INSPIRED BY THE CHESHIRE CAT,
ALICE IN WONDERLAND

T HE INITIAL USE Cases I've talked about are intended
to provide a foundational toolbox of potential analyses
to address various challenges within your organization. I
hope that learning about these Use Cases has inspired you
to start working with CBM to bring clarity in making and
communicating strategic decisions. As a relatively new field,
there is still much ground to explore in CBM, and numerous
additional Use Cases can be investigated and formalized for
future application.

The Use Cases discussed previously are merely valuable
steps in the complex puzzle of the Strategic Management

and Enterprise Architecture practice. Developing a good strategy is neither linear, nor purely sequential. Therefore, in this chapter we will explore various scenarios in which organizations face specific challenges, and the Use Cases that can be employed to help tackle them. The scenarios presented are tested (and researched) at least once, but are still quite new.

In Chapter 6, I offer my view on future possibilities for the CBM practice. My aim is to spark interest among other practitioners and researchers and encourage them to contribute to the development and practice of CBM. As this is ongoing research, treat this chapter and the next as inspiration for what can be achieved, rather than as an exact or mature science.

A final note on these scenarios is that they often occur simultaneously. Organizations typically have multiple initiatives running concurrently. By steering all these initiatives through the lens of CBM, we can better understand their impact on the organization and each other. This approach allows for improved alignment and decision-making, ultimately enhancing the overall outcome.

5.1   SCENARIO: Digital Transformation

First, we will cover the scenario of digital transformation. Various definitions of "digital transformation" exist, as investigated and described by Gregory Vial from HEC Montréal and others [34, 35]. One common theme is that digital transformations trigger significant organizational change that involves the introduction of digital products and services, and substantially impacts how organizations operate [36]. While transformation always involves a shift from a current to a future state, digital transformation specifically relies

on the use of combinations of new information, comput-
ing, communication, and connectivity technologies, known
as "digital technologies."

At the time of writing, we are conducting an ongoing
study in this field to discover and describe how CBM can
help organize and execute digital transformations [37].
The main idea behind this study is to examine the different building blocks of digital transformation, as identified
by Gregory Vial [34], and observe how organizations use
CBM Use Cases to manage these building blocks. Below is
an overview of the different phases, based on Vial's study,
which helps us understand the dynamics of digital transformation at an organizational level. The image has been
adapted to reflect bi-directional relationships between the
phases, and provide simplification on one hand and additional nuance on the other.

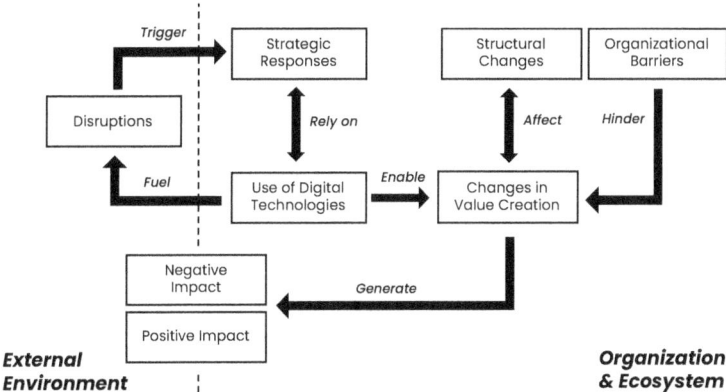

FIGURE 5.1 The phases of digital
transformation, adapted from Vial [34]

The phases of digital transformation (according to Vial)

Disruptions: This stage includes changes in consumer behavior and expectations, a competitive landscape, and the availability of data, all fueled by digital technologies.

Strategic responses: Organizations develop a digital business strategy and a digital transformation strategy in response to these disruptions. These strategic responses are triggered by disruptions and influenced by the availability of innovative solutions.

Use of digital technologies: Organizations utilize various digital technologies such as social media, mobile technology, analytics, the Internet of Things (IoT), and platforms and ecosystems to address disruptions. The use of these technologies often results from strategic choices.

Changes in value creation: The adoption of these technologies leads to changes in value creation pathways, including value propositions, value networks, digital channels, and organizational agility and ambidexterity. Organizations can start creating value in different ways, either through the products and services they offer or in how they create and deliver them.

Structural changes: Changes in value creation lead to structural modifications within the organization, such as shifts in organizational structure, culture, leadership, and employee roles and skills, as well as in relationships with partners.

Organizational barriers: These transformations often encounter organizational barriers like inertia and resistance, which hinder organizational change.

Impacts: These changes generate various impacts. Negative impacts include security and privacy concerns, while positive impacts encompass improved operational efficiency, enhanced organizational performance, and broader industry and societal improvements. Impacts are felt within the organization and its immediate ecosystem, as well as in the broader external environment.

Our research has provided initial evidence that specific Use Cases can help manage these building blocks. Below, you see a first mapping between the Use Cases presented in this book and the digital transformation building blocks covered earlier. While this is an ongoing study and the results are preliminary (and so might change or be expanded), they are nonetheless interesting. By applying CBM and these specific Use Cases to manage the different aspects of a digital transformation, you could improve your digital transformation endeavor.

5.1.1   Strategic Response

A robust strategic response is critical for navigating the complexities of digital transformation. Several Use Cases provide substantial support in shaping and aligning this response:

- **USE CASE 1: Strategic Emphasis through Motivation Modeling** helps shape the digital transformation plan by providing insights into which capabilities are crucial (direct and supporting) for realizing the digital transformation ambitions, thus facilitating alignment.

- **USE CASE 5: Fit-Gap Analysis** supports the creation of a phased digital transformation plan by presenting the outcomes of a gap analysis, highlighting areas that need attention.

- **USE CASE 7: Capability Integration and Standardization Profiles (CISPS)** aids in shaping the digital transformation plan by facilitating the necessary organizational choices to achieve digital transformation ambitions. This is particularly relevant in larger organizations where capabilities span multiple subsidiaries. Decisions related to integration and standardization will help determine the organization's future structure. Consequently, this approach allows for a more complete and holistic strategic view of what the transformation will mean for the organization.

5.1.2   Digital Technologies

The integration of digital technologies is a cornerstone of digital transformation, though it is often discussed indirectly:

- **USE CASE 1: Strategic Emphasis through Motivation Modeling** indirectly supports digital technology integration. While not always immediately visible, certain IT and data capabilities are prerequisites for leveraging digital technology, which is crucial for realizing digital transformation ambitions. Identifying these capabilities is a vital part of the analysis.

- **USE CASE 4: Operational Resource Mapping** supports technology integration by identifying the current technology used for specific capabilities and mapping new technologies onto them. Additionally, it helps map the required information for these new technologies to function properly (garbage in, garbage out). By understanding which roles (people) will be impacted by the introduction of new technologies, we can assess potential competency shifts and plan for reskilling, upskilling, or increasing staffing levels.

- **USE CASE 5: Fit-Gap Analysis** directly involves assessing technology, indicating which areas are underperforming against the desired future state to be achieved after the digital transformation.

- **USE CASE 7: Capability Integration and Standardization Profiles (CISPS)** also offers indirect support. New and existing technologies must be evaluated for standardization and integration. When a new technology can be leveraged across multiple subsidiaries, the business case becomes significantly more advantageous.

5.1.3   Value Creation Paths

Value creation paths are essential for defining how an organization generates and captures value:

- **USE CASE 4: Operational Resource Mapping** aids in identifying and understanding the operational dimensions that directly impact value creation paths. These paths are facilitated by different capabilities and the operational resources connected to them.

- **USE CASE 5: Fit-Gap Analysis** supports this by providing a gap status on capabilities and the underlying key processes, aiding decision-making on value creation paths. Use Case 4 serves as a crucial prerequisite for this analysis.

- **USE CASE 7: Capability Integration and Standardization Profiles (CISPS)** indirectly supports analyzing and managing value creation paths. Decisions made at the capability level impact the underlying processes and other operational resources, thereby influencing how value creation paths are operationalized. Choices regarding integration or standardization will significantly affect these paths.

5.1.4   Structural Changes

Digital transformation often necessitates significant structural changes within the organization:

- **USE CASE 1: Strategic Emphasis through Motivation Modeling** helps identify key capabilities for the digital transformation. These capabilities are earmarked for thorough analysis and potential substantial change, or must be sourced. This is a crucial first step in making decisions about organizational structures and culture, as well as the skills and competencies required for successful digital transformation and relationships with partners.

- **USE CASE 5: Fit-Gap Analysis** provides insights related to competencies and the availability of employees, derived from a gap analysis on the capability and people dimensions.

- **USE CASE 7: Capability Integration and Standardization Profiles (CISPs)** aids in decisions on organizational structures, such as central versus decentralized approaches (prerequisites for subsequent transformation stages), and will impact how the organization is structured.

5.1.5   Organizational Barriers

Overcoming organizational barriers is vital for the success of digital transformation initiatives:

- **USE CASE 1: Strategic Emphasis through Motivation Modeling** helps initiate discussions about necessary changes and creates awareness among key stakeholders.

- **USE CASE 7: Capability Integration and Standardization Profiles (CISPs)** supports by starting discussions about what needs to change and raising awareness among stakeholders.

- **USE CASE 5: Fit-Gap Analysis** contributes by facilitating discussions on changes and creating awareness among key stakeholders.

5.1.6   Other Use Cases

Even though Use Cases 2, 3, 6, and 8 were not included in the initial study, they will undoubtedly contribute to the success of a digital transformation endeavor. After all, a digital transformation is an organization-wide strategic program and cannot be viewed independently from other strategic programs and decisions.

- **USE CASE 8: Accountability and Responsibility Assignment** is likely the easiest to grasp, as assigning clear responsibilities facilitates decision-making and ensures results.

- **USE CASE 3: SWOT Analysis for Capabilities** can identify weaknesses that might hinder the achievement of digital transformation objectives. These insights can then be factored into decision-making and solution-building processes.

- **USE CASE 6: Outsourcing** might reveal valid choices within the scope of digital transformation objectives where outsourcing is the optimal strategy to meet requirements. By clearly understanding which capabilities have been outsourced and to what extent, we can better assess the potential impact on our future organizational design.

- **USE CASE 2: Strategic Profiles for Capabilities** provides a clear view of the relative position of certain capabilities. Although digital transformation can alter this vision, it remains crucial to consider when making transformation decisions. For instance, if a highly standardized capability needs to become differentiated or even innovative, explicitly stating this change helps us better understand the impact and the necessary adjustments.

5.2   SCENARIO: Green Transformation
Co-author: Dr. Ing. Niels Vandevenne

Earlier, we introduced a comprehensive framework for digital transformation (as articulated by Vial) comprised of eight building blocks, and discussed digital transformation (or DT) and how we can apply CBM to improve its outcome. One critical and often underexplored aspect in the context of DT is sustainability. In this scenario, the focus lies on environmental sustainability (ES), which involves responsible natural resource management to meet current needs without compromising future generations [38].

As with all strategic initiatives and topics, sustainability and DT are not mutually exclusive. In fact, they can be highly complementary, and should be considered as two sides of the same coin. Integrating sustainability efforts with DT can lead to significant environmental benefits and help resolve the contradiction between economic growth and environmental quality [39]. Moreover, embedding sustainability into an organization's value proposition can distinguish it from competitors (related to Use Case 2: Strategic Profiles for Capabilities), enhancing its appeal to customers and employees [2].

ES takes center stage

Despite the evident synergies, sustainability is unfortunately absent from many (if not most) DT frameworks, including Vial's. Although the importance of ethical considerations such as corporate social responsibility is often acknowledged, the connection between ES and DT warrants a more explicit emphasis. After all, ES is likely to be one of the major topics on most organizations' strategic agendas in the next decade.

This is where CBM can play a pivotal role. By using CBM, organizations can systematically align their DT (and other) efforts with their sustainability goals. CBM helps identify, develop, and optimize capabilities that are crucial for achieving digital and sustainable transformations. Through CBM, organizations can:

1 **Identify, define, and implement core ES capabilities**: Inspired by the ES research and practice domain, specific capabilities can be identified that are crucial to the ES initiative and for integrating ES with DT. Identifying and setting up (or sourcing) these capabilities can present an important step forward in becoming an ES organization. Examples are capabilities such as ESG (Environmental, Social, and Governance) reporting and Green Strategy Definition.

2 **Identify key sustainability drivers**: Understand what drives the organization's sustainability goals and how these drivers align with DT initiatives.

3 **Define tangible sustainability goals**: Set clear, measurable sustainability targets integrated into the broader (digital) transformation strategy.

4 **Map requirements to capabilities**: Determine the specific requirements needed to achieve sustainability goals and map these to the organization's capabilities.

5 **Analyze and optimize capabilities**: Conduct Fit-Gap analyses to identify which capabilities need enhancement or innovation to meet sustainability targets.

Put simply, there are two main aspects of how CBM can improve ES in organizations. The first focuses on developing new capabilities crucial to the ES initiative. These not only facilitate the realization of an ES-aware organization, but also allow that organization to integrate an ES initiative with potential DT initiatives.

The second aspect centers on analyzing, assessing, and enhancing the "green" side of existing capabilities. By defining and evaluating relevant green drivers and indicators of current capabilities, organizations can ensure that their operations better contribute to ES practices. We refer to these indicators as Key Environmental Performance Indicators (KEPIS)—similar to KPIS, but specifically focused on the ES dimension of an organization.

Environmental sustainability as an initiative can be a driver. However, by integrating sustainability into the core of DT through CBM, organizations can ensure that their digital initiatives are not only transformative from an organizational point of view, but also environmentally responsible. This holistic approach fosters innovation and efficiency and contributes to a sustainable future, aligning the organization's growth with environmental stewardship.

Let's go color-coded

Below is a fictional case study of how this can be presented on a Capability Map. The creation (or sourcing) of ES-specific capabilities is like that of any other capability. For example, strategic profiles (SP) and Capability Integration and Standardization Profiles (CISPs) need to be assigned, responsibilities defined, and a gap analysis performed. As for the KEPIS, these can be defined similarly to KPIS, but warrant their own indicators on the CapMap.

This is shown in figure 5.2 (below), where a leaf icon is added to each capability to represent its KEPI status. Each

KEPI must have one or more measurable targets. If multiple KEPIS are defined for a capability, determine how they are weighted against each other and how they can be integrated into an overall ES-related score for a capability. The color of the indicator—according to, e.g., a three-level Red-Amber-Green (or RAG) scheme—reflects how well the organization is meeting its ES targets for these capabilities.

In this example, multiple levels were set for each KEPI (or set of KEPIS) for a capability: Red (dark gray) indicates severely underperforming; Amber (medium gray) indicates slightly underperforming; and Green (white) means the target is met. Naturally, the specific targets must be clearly defined. Black indicates that no KEPI was defined for a capability or that no measurable target was set. So, for example, when it comes to Data and Information Management, the organization is meeting the targets put forward. However, for Infrastructure Management, an outsourced capability (note the "O" indicator), targets are not met. This indicates that a conversation with the provider of this capability is required.

Indicating KEPIs

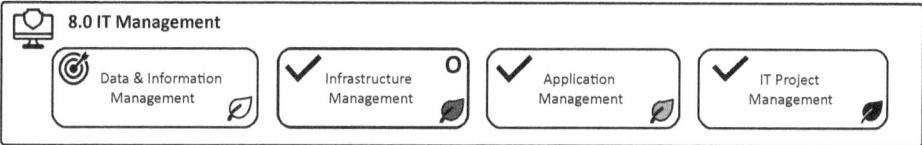

FIGURE 5.2 Indicating the current KEPI score
for specific capabilities in an organization

Let's consider a more detailed example where the GREAN framework is used to enhance the sustainability of the two specific capabilities mentioned above: Infrastructure Management, and Data and Information Management. To measure and develop these capabilities, KEPIS are proposed which require a certain level of capability maturity, as outlined in Use Case 0.

For the Data and Information Management capability, KEPIS are defined for each operational dimension and scored using a Red-Amber-Green (RAG) scale, where Green indicates that the target level for a specific dimension has been met. Threshold values are set to determine when the score transitions from Red to Amber to Green. As mentioned, to effectively measure and track these KEPIS, an appropriate capability maturity level is essential. Measurement requires a solid level of control over the operational dimensions—so, in this case, the capability maturity level should be at least 3 (Defined and Documented), and preferably 4 (Measured and Controlled), for the relevant parts of the capability. However, note that this does not mean every process within the capability needs to be managed at Level 4 according to the Business Process Maturity framework.

The table below shows the KEPIS for the Data and Information Management capability. Three of the four dimensions have a Green score, while the process dimension scores Amber. The overall capability KEPI score in this case is Green, indicating good compliance with the set environmental objectives. No further initiatives are needed to enhance environmental sustainability for this capability. However, an optional initiative is identified for the process dimension to bring it to a Green score as well.

Values ▶ Dimension ▼	Red – Amber	Amber – Green	Actual Score	Explanation of Actual Score	Suggested Initiatives
People	<20%	20-40%	Green	40% awareness level of data management staff regarding green data practices.	N.a.
Processes	<30%	30-50%	Amber	40% of data governed by green data life cycle management.	8. Assess and implement environmentally sustainable data patterns in the data architecture and lifecycle management.
Information	<40%	40-60%	Green	60% quality of data on the environmental impact of data management practices.	N.a.
Technology	<20%	20-40%	Green	40% implementation rate of green data management technologies.	N.a.

FIGURE 5.3 KEPIS of Data and Information Management

For Infrastructure Management, KEPIS are defined across the four capability dimensions—People, Processes, Information, and Technology—but no threshold values have been set. Since this capability is outsourced here, setting specific KEPIS and scoring them may not be feasible. The configuration of these dimensions is outside the control and responsibility of the enterprise. However, certain expectations can be set for the supplier to demonstrate their sustainability practices, allowing the enterprise to assign a Green score if sufficient proof is provided by the supplier. The table below presents an overview of these expectations for each dimension.

Dimension	Expectations from supplier
People	Have people certified in green Infrastructure practices. E.g. apply public cloud training, patterns, and tools to assess and optimise carbon footprint and electricity usage.
Processes	Certifications in environmental sustainability frameworks and standards. Apply a Green IT maturity model focussed on green IT infrastructure.
Information	Be able to present complete and correct information on overall energy consumption and CO2 impact of the enterprise's workloads.
Technology	Prefer to compute in the public cloud rather than onpremises. Continuously identify opportunities for greener IT resources and be able to present a green roadmap for the next 5 years.

FIGURE 5.4 Supplier expectations for Infrastructure Management

It is also important to recognize that not all capabilities need to achieve the same level of Environmental Sustainability. Capabilities that are designated for a lower level of ES maturity could score Green, while those intended for a higher level might score Amber, even though the latter may exhibit better ES practices in absolute terms. This differentiation allows the organization to prioritize capabilities based on their strategic importance. By setting realistic targets, the organization avoids aiming too high across multiple capabilities simultaneously. Ultimately, a Green score signifies that the organization is meeting its targets, not necessarily that it's best-in-class.

5.3   SCENARIO: Carve-out

When it comes to corporate restructuring, carve-outs present a unique set of challenges, essentially requiring the disentanglement of a subsidiary from its parent organization, a reverse process to that of mergers and acquisitions. In a previous case (which I can't disclose here), we leveraged CBM to facilitate a carve-out for an organization, allowing us to investigate the power of this approach in managing such complex scenarios.

At the heart of this carve-out was the need to comprehensively understand the interdependencies between the parent organization and the other subsidiaries on one hand, and the subsidiary to be carved out on the other hand, across various dimensions, including Processes, Information, People, and Applications. Using the capability structure as our guiding framework, we meticulously mapped out these interdependencies to gain a clear picture of the ties that needed to be addressed.

One of the critical steps involved identifying which capabilities were supported by applications owned and maintained by the subsidiary, but also used across other parts (subsidiaries and HQ) of the organization. By mapping these applications to their respective capabilities, we could pinpoint exactly where the technological dependencies lay. This insight was crucial for determining what needed to be transferred to another part of the organization or replicated to ensure continuity of operations post-carve-out. The same was done for the reverse case: what applications were supporting the subsidiary in focus?

Information is power

Similarly, we conducted an in-depth analysis of information flows, identifying capabilities that relied on data shared between the subsidiary and other organizational units. Understanding these information dependencies allowed us to plan for data migration, replication, or the establishment of new data-sharing agreements to maintain the integrity and availability of critical information.

We also mapped People and Process dependencies which involved identifying key personnel and process roles within the subsidiary that were integral to the broader organization's operations. By understanding these HR and process interconnections, we could plan for the necessary transfers, training, or hiring to fill any gaps the carve-out would create.

The image below (figure 5.5) illustrates how this can be represented on a CapMap. In this example, the CapMap of subsidiary X (the entity being carved out) is the foundation. We denote which capabilities are provided by subsidiary X to the headquarters (HQ) or other subsidiaries, which is crucial because replacements must be arranged for these capabilities. Conversely, we identify which capabilities are "consumed" by subsidiary X, meaning they were partially or fully provided by HQ or another subsidiary. This indication is valuable for two main reasons: first, it highlights that subsidiary X will no longer utilize these capabilities, necessitating actions such as severing access to applications and downscaling capacity on the provider's side; second, it is pertinent for either the acquiring party of subsidiary X, or subsidiary X itself if it is to operate independently, as they would have to answer the same questions in the reverse.

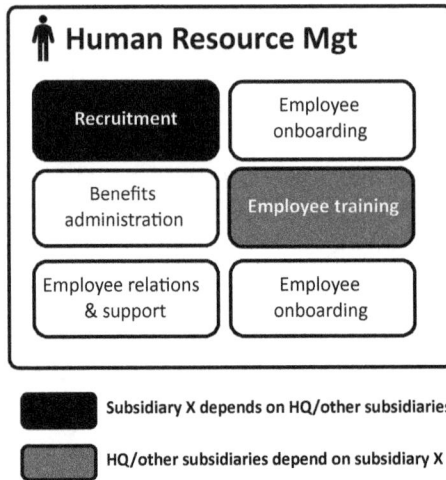

FIGURE 5.5 Indicating the dependencies between subsidiaries on a Capability Map

In some cases, the Capability Integration and Standardization Profiles (CISP) centralization was applied. Here, the subsidiary functioned as an outsourcing partner, providing specialized capabilities to HQ or other subsidiaries. These instances required careful consideration of how these capabilities would be managed post-carve-out (either outsourced to a new provider, or internalized within the remaining organization).

The culmination of this Capability Mapping and analysis provided a comprehensive view of all operational ties. This holistic understanding was pivotal in developing a detailed plan for the carve-out, outlining what needed to be transferred, replicated, or established to achieve clean separation. Using CBM in this context not only facilitated the carve-out, but also ensured that the parent organization could continue its operations seamlessly and with minimal disruption. Based on only one practice experience, the case in question already sparked optimism for applying CBM in such a situation.

5.4   SCENARIO: Mergers and Acquisitions (M&A)

Mergers and acquisitions (M&A) are strategic moves aimed at enhancing a firm's competitive position, expanding its market reach, or acquiring new capabilities. However, the success of M&A largely depends on how well the merging entities can integrate their operations and strategic objectives. Here, CBM offers a powerful framework to navigate the complexities of M&A, ensuring that the integration is smooth, strategic, and value-creating.

In an M&A scenario, the acquiring company is not just obtaining tangible assets and a customer portfolio; it is also acquiring a set of capabilities that the target company possesses. CBM, as presented in this book, provides a structured approach to assess and compare the capabilities of both organizations. By mapping out the capabilities of each entity, it becomes possible to identify overlaps, gaps, and unique strengths. This comparative analysis helps in making informed decisions about which capabilities to retain, integrate, or further develop.

One of the critical challenges in M&A is integrating similar capabilities from both organizations after the merger or acquisition. CBM facilitates this by providing a clear framework to evaluate and decide which capability will be the leading template (or kept in case of a full integration) in the new, combined entity. In case only one instance of certain (or all) capabilities can be kept, because we are fully integrating two organizations into one, we need to decide which will be kept. The example below illustrates how this could be indicated on a CapMap.

Indicating Leading Capability (M&A)

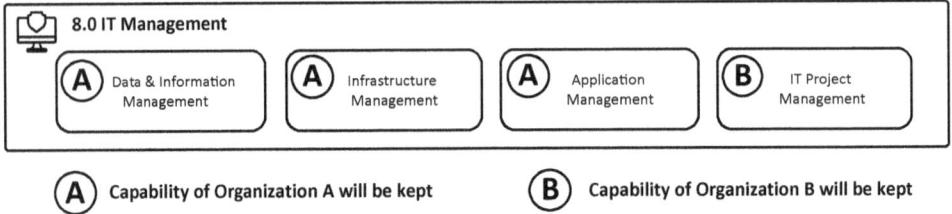

FIGURE 5.6 Indicating on a CapMap which capability instance will be kept in an M&A full-integration scenario

This analysis involves further understanding the strategic profile (SP, as presented in Use Case 2) of the involved capabilities and how they were organized from an operational point-of-view. The SP indicates the strategic importance and future potential assigned to each capability. This understanding allows us to determine whether, for example, the inbound logistics capability of Organization A is being developed similarly (e.g., being standardized) to how this same capability is being developed in Organization B. If discrepancies are found, it signals potential challenges in integrating these capabilities or helps us decide which one to keep (if we can't keep both). The Capability Integration and Standardization Profiles (CISPs) will then play a crucial role in realizing the acquisition or merger, especially if the two entities are not fully integrated into one. In such cases, duplicate capabilities must be organized effectively, and assigning a CISP will help determine the necessary degree of integration and standardization. This structured approach ensures that both overlapping and unique capabilities are managed to support the strategic goals of the newly formed entity.

In line for alignment

So, as per the above, CBM helps assess the compatibility of the merging entities. By analyzing the existing capabilities and their strategic alignment, organizations can gauge whether their combined strengths will create synergy or lead to conflicts. This involves looking at the capabilities of both organizations to understand how well their capabilities align with each other and with the overarching strategic goals of the new entity. To ensure a successful integration, map out how the capabilities of both organizations interact on various levels (Processes, Information, People, and Applications) and compare these to each other to better understand the challenge ahead.

A thorough study on this has been described by Andreas Freitag in his PhD thesis "Applying Business Capabilities in a Corporate Buyer M&A Process" [40]. He underscores the significance of Enterprise Architecture Management (EAM) and business capabilities in M&A. Freitag emphasizes that EAM provides a strategic framework to align business and IT resources, ensuring that both are harmonized during the M&A process. His research highlights the common challenges in M&A, such as inadequate integration processes and misalignment of business strategies, and proposes solutions based on better planning and execution of business capabilities.

5.5   SCENARIO: Quality Management System

In traditional quality management systems (QMS) such as ISO, the emphasis is typically placed on processes, with controls and indicators established at the process level to ensure quality standards are met. While this has merit, I strongly advocate for adopting a capability focus first. By doing so, we can unlock significant advantages that are often overlooked in conventional QMS implementations.

A capability focus allows us to define controls and indicators at the capability level before delving into specific processes. This approach offers a holistic view of the organization, aligning quality metrics with broader strategic objectives and facilitating a more integrated and adaptable quality management framework. One of the primary benefits of this method is the reusability of the capability structure. Once capabilities are defined and mapped, they provide a stable foundation that can be utilized across various domains, including QMS, operational management, and CBM initiatives.

By linking QMS metrics to capabilities, organizations can ensure that quality indicators are not only process-specific, but also aligned with the strategic importance of the capabilities they support. This linkage facilitates a comprehensive understanding of how quality impacts overall business performance and strategic goals. For instance, a capability such as Product Development can have quality indicators related to innovation, time-to-market, and customer satisfaction. These indicators can then be broken down into specific process metrics, but their alignment with the capability ensures that quality management supports the broader strategic intent.

A novel take on QMS

Moreover, this capability-first approach provides flexibility in adapting to changes. As business environments evolve and new capabilities emerge or existing ones transform, the quality metrics can be adjusted at the capability level, ensuring that quality management remains relevant and aligned with current strategic priorities. This adaptability is often more challenging in a process-first approach, where changes at the process level can become cumbersome and disjointed.

Incorporating a capability focus also enhances the integration of QMS with other CBM-related choices. When capabilities serve as the primary lens through which quality is managed, it becomes easier to align quality metrics with other operational dimensions, such as resource allocation, technology deployment, and organizational structure. This fosters a more cohesive and efficient management system, where quality management is inherently linked to overall business performance and strategic direction.

As QMS is mostly a thought experiment based on limited practical experience and not founded on scientific research, shifting to a capability focus in QMS seems to offer a more robust, flexible, and strategically aligned approach to quality management. It ensures that quality controls and indicators are not only process-specific, but also integrated into the broader organizational framework, thus enhancing the overall effectiveness and adaptability of the QMS. By leveraging the stability and reusability of the capability structure, organizations can achieve a more comprehensive and cohesive quality management system that supports continuous improvement and strategic success. So, even though this is a rather novel take on QMS—and I don't suggest that the process level is not relevant anymore for QMS—it's well worth looking into.

CHAPTER 6

LOOKING FORWARD
Expanding the Horizons of CBM

"The best way to predict the future is to create it."

PETER DRUCKER

6.1 Governance, good practices, and audit

A significant advantage of managing an organization based on its capabilities is the enhanced governance it provides. A well-defined capability structure allows for clearer ownership and accountability across the organization. By explicitly assigning ownership of capabilities and, consequently, the underlying operating models, organizations can better delineate responsibilities and improve oversight. This clarity also extends to audits, making it easier to translate expectations to specific capabilities and their underlying processes, roles, and applications, thereby facilitating more targeted and effective reporting.

Elevating the capability structure and map can significantly improve audit processes. It provides a transparent

161

framework that auditors can use to assess whether the organization meets its governance standards. Expectations can be directly linked to specific capabilities, ensuring that all relevant aspects are comprehensively covered. This structured approach not only simplifies the audit process, but also enhances the organization's ability to adopt industry or domain-specific governance models.

In our research with football clubs and national football federations, we explore how a capability structure can serve as the foundation for a good-practices framework that can collect and share good practices for different capabilities, enabling teams to learn from each other and even benchmark their performance (if so desired). By using a consistent capability model for governance and auditing, we can create robust frameworks that not only prepare them for audits, but also drive continuous improvement.

Furthermore, the use of capability-based governance models allows for better alignment with strategic goals. It ensures that every capability—and, by extension, every process and role—is optimized to support the organization's objectives. This alignment can be particularly beneficial in industries with stringent regulatory requirements, where adherence to best practices is critical for compliance and operational excellence.

Image 6.1 illustrates a structured framework for managing the Safety Management capability in a football club, aligning it with governance and audit requirements. This framework used three key components as dimensions for the framework—Capability Goals, Key Processes, and Key Roles. For each capability goal, such as "keeping the number of safety-related incidents during game-day events as low as possible" or "providing fans with a safe feeling," related metrics like the "number of incidents" and "number of reported safety issues" are defined to measure performance. The maturity or audit levels specify the expected values or benchmarks for these metrics.

Capability goal	Related metrics	Maturity/audit levels
Keep number of safety related incidents during gameday events as low as possible	■ Number of incidents ■ ..	Expected number/value
Provide fans with a safe feeling	■ Number of reported safety issues ■ ..	

Key processes	Critical steps/activities	Maturity/audit levels
Maintain safety procedures	Step 1. (Minimal outcome) Step 2. (Minimal outcome) (In a later phase, draw high-level process models)	What level is required by the governing body?
Security staff planning	..	..
Provide safety 'hotline'	...	..

Key roles	Role description	Maturity/audit levels
Chief security officer	Description and key competencies + responsibilities	What roles are required by the governing body?

FIGURE 6.1 Exploring possible dimensions and values
for a good practices and audit framework for football clubs

Key processes integral to this capability, such as maintaining safety procedures, security staff planning, and providing a safety hotline, are broken down into critical steps or activities, with corresponding maturity or audit levels indicating the required standards set by governing bodies. Maintaining safety procedures, for example, involves specified steps to achieve minimal outcomes, aligning with the standards mandated by regulatory authorities. Finally, key roles like Chief Security Officer are outlined, with role descriptions detailing their responsibilities and competencies. The maturity or audit levels here define the roles required by the governing body, ensuring that all organizational responsibilities are clearly understood and met. This comprehensive model integrates capability management with governance and audit practices, fostering an environment of continuous improvement and accountability.

6.2   Integration with cost accounting

Another potentially promising direction for future research and practical application lies in integrating the capability structure with cost accounting practices. Traditionally, cost accounting relies on cost allocation methods to accurately assign costs to the appropriate domains within an organization. However, this can often become complex and convoluted, especially in large organizations with diverse operations.

Integrating cost accounting with CBM could offer a structured approach that streamlines this complexity. By leveraging the capability structure as a foundational framework for cost allocation, organizations can achieve a more precise and transparent understanding of their cost dynamics. In a CBM framework, each capability represents a distinct function or set of activities within the organization. These can be mapped out in a hierarchical structure, detailing the various levels of operational execution. By aligning cost accounting methods with this capability hierarchy, costs can be allocated more accurately and meaningfully. This includes both operational and capital expenditures.

Think about a Marketing capability in an organization. The costs associated with Marketing activities—campaign management, customer engagement, market research, and so on—can be directly linked to the specific capabilities responsible for these activities. This link not only provides a clearer picture of where resources are being utilized, but also helps in identifying areas for potential cost optimization.

Moreover, integrating cost accounting with CBM can facilitate better decision-making. When costs are aligned with capabilities, it's easier to assess the financial impact of strategic decisions, such as expanding a particular capability, investing in new technologies, or scaling down underperforming areas. This alignment allows for a more granular analysis of cost efficiency and effectiveness across different parts of the organization.

6.3   New startup

Starting a new organization is an exhilarating, but challenging, endeavor. It's marked by numerous difficulties that can overwhelm even the most experienced founders. One critical aspect of launching a successful startup is to ensure that all necessary functions (or capabilities) are properly developed or sourced. The challenge is twofold: to identify all relevant capabilities, and also to determine which ones to prioritize and deploy first.

CBM offers a structured approach that can significantly benefit startups in navigating such complex terrain. By leveraging a well-defined capability structure, startup founders can avoid the pitfalls of having to invent everything from scratch and instead focus on strategically planning and prioritizing their efforts.

Identifying Relevant Capabilities: For any startup, the first step is to comprehensively identify the capabilities required to achieve its strategic objectives. This involves considering all aspects of the business, from core operations and marketing to support functions such as HR and IT. CBM could provide a reference framework (generic or industry-specific) that outlines these capabilities in a hierarchical structure, making it easier for founders to visualize and understand the full spectrum of what needs to be accomplished.

For example, a technology startup might identify capabilities such as Product Development, Customer Support, Sales, and Marketing. Each of these high-level capabilities can then be broken down into more specific functions, such as software engineering, user experience design, lead generation, and customer relationship management. By mapping out these capabilities, founders gain a clear picture of the essential building blocks of their business.

Prioritizing and Planning: Once the relevant capabilities are identified, the next challenge is to prioritize and plan their development or sourcing. This is where CBM truly shines. By providing a structured approach, CBM helps startups allocate their limited resources (time, money, and talent) more effectively. Startup founders can use the capability structure to determine which capabilities are critical to achieving immediate goals and which can be developed over time. For instance, in the early stages a startup might prioritize capabilities related to product development and initial market entry, while planning to enhance capabilities such as customer support and operational scaling as the business grows.

Strategic Decision-Making: CBM also aids in strategic decision-making by highlighting interdependencies between capabilities and potential areas for leveraging external resources. For instance, a startup might decide to outsource non-core capabilities, such as accounting or IT support, to focus on core activities that drive competitive advantage. Additionally, understanding the strategic profile (SP) of each capability helps founders align their efforts with the long-term vision of the organization.

In practical terms, startups can implement CBM by developing a CapMap that outlines all identified capabilities and their respective priorities. This map serves as a dynamic tool for planning, execution, and monitoring progress. It provides a visual representation of the business's functional landscape, enabling founders to make informed decisions and adjust their strategies as the company evolves.

6.4   Event planning and management

Planning and running events, whether corporate conferences, music festivals, sports tournaments or any number of other examples, involves a multitude of tasks that require meticulous coordination and execution. CBM offers a structured framework that can greatly enhance the planning and operational efficiency of events. By defining all necessary capabilities and their operational dimensions, event organizers can ensure comprehensive preparation, effective staffing, and a high-quality experience for attendees. Additionally, applying strategic profiles (SPS) to these capabilities can help determine which aspects of the event should be standardized, differentiated, or innovated.

Defining event capabilities and operational dimensions: The first step in applying CBM to event management is to identify and define the capabilities required for the event. These encompass all aspects of planning, execution, and post-event activities, and each involves various operational dimensions, including Processes, People (roles), Information, and Applications/Technology. By defining these dimensions, event organizers can ensure that every aspect of the event is covered and adequately prepared. For example:

- **Processes**: Detailed workflows for each capability, such as the steps involved in coordinating speakers or managing on-site logistics.

- **People**: Specific roles and responsibilities for team members, such as event coordinators, marketing managers, and technical support staff.

- **Information**: The critical data and documentation needed, such as attendee lists, vendor contracts, and marketing materials.

- **Applications/Technology**: Tools and platforms required to support each capability, such as event management software, ticketing systems, and audiovisual equipment.

Strategic profile (SP): Applying the SP Use Case to event capabilities can further refine the planning and execution process. By determining which capabilities should be standardized, differentiated, or innovated, event organizers can allocate resources more effectively and enhance the overall event experience, as per the outline below (note that the "Differentiated capabilities" reference below can mean both output and cost differentiation).

- **Standardized capabilities**: Capabilities should follow industry norms and best practices to ensure consistency and reliability. For example, basic registration processes and catering services can be standardized.

- **Differentiated capabilities**: Capabilities that provide a competitive advantage and unique value proposition. For instance, personalized attendee services or a unique marketing campaign can differentiate the event from others.

- **Innovative capabilities**: Capabilities that involve experimenting with new ideas and approaches to create a memorable and distinctive experience. Examples include interactive technology installations, novel session formats, or cutting-edge entertainment options.

So, in practice, event organizers can create a Capability Map that visualizes all identified capabilities and their operational dimensions. This map serves as a dynamic tool for planning, executing, and monitoring event activities. By applying CBM, organizers can ensure that each capability is adequately prepared, staffed, and executed to meet strategic goals.

Additionally, assigning an SP to each capability helps prioritize efforts and resources, ensuring that the event achieves its intended impact. For example, if audience engagement is identified as a key differentiator, resources can be allocated to innovative engagement techniques, while standardized processes handle routine tasks efficiently.

CONCLUSION

AS YOU HAVE SEEN, I am very enthusiastic about the possibilities and future potential of Capability-Based Management. I hope you now share that enthusiasm after reading this book. I believe CBM can evolve into a robust management method for analyzing and steering organizations.

However, a critical concern—one that is also highlighted by several scholars [41, 42]—is the absence of a universally accepted definition and a standardized framework for the Capability concept and Capability Maps. This lack of consensus not only hampers academic research, but also impedes broader acceptance and quality of application in practice. The existing plurality of interpretations regarding what constitutes a capability fosters ambiguity and misalignment, undermining the potential and effectiveness of CBM.

CBM on the road to growth

For CBM to be recognized as a key Enterprise Architecture practice—with the concept of Capability at its core facilitating enhanced decision-making—it is imperative to establish an unambiguous and widely embraced definition.

The development of grounded, well-researched methods for defining and utilizing Capability Maps—a central pillar of CBM practice—greatly depends on the clarity and consensus around the foundational concept of Capability. In response to this need for a more solid foundation for the Capability concept and its applications, the International Workshop on the Foundations and Applications of Capabilities in Enterprises, Transformations, and ESG Initiatives (FACETE) was initiated. Its focus is to bring academics and practitioners to the table and find a consensus that will help us to grow CBM's maturity.

This book represents what we (I) know up to now, but does not mark the end of growing the practice. Therefore, I strongly encourage academics and practitioners alike to adopt and improve CBM and contribute to its knowledge base. Feel free to reach out. You can visit www.capmap.org or www.facete.org to get in touch or learn more about what we do and find the latest updates. Or, you can find me at LinkedIn or ResearchGate.

Ready to take Capability-Based Management further? Visit www.capmap.org to explore training opportunities, connect with the community, and access free resources. You'll find high-resolution versions of the book's examples, templates to build your own CapMap, and additional materials to help you apply CBM in your organization.

Thank you so much for reading the book. I hope it gives you greater knowledge to help you tackle your professional challenges.

APPENDIX
Use Case Repository
(Short Descriptions)

CBM USE CASE 1: Strategic Emphasis through Motivation Modeling

Objective: Determine which capabilities will be crucial for realizing the strategic ambitions of the organization.

Process:

1 **Identify strategic drivers:** Start from the organization's vision and mission to determine what drives the realization of these elements. Break down drivers into more granular drivers to understand the detailed aspects that influence the strategic vision.

2 **Define tangible goals:** Translate these drivers into specific, measurable goals that are clear and tangible, with set targets, percentages, or numbers.

3 **Determine requirements:** Identify the requirements needed to achieve these goals. Bridge the gap between strategic goals and the operational steps needed to achieve them.

4 **Link to capabilities:** Identify which capabilities are relevant to meet and implement these requirements. This step ensures that the strategic vision is translated into actionable capabilities.

Outcome:
- Highlight key capabilities on the Capability Map by indicating different levels of priority or using visual markers.

- Revisit this analysis after conducting Fit-Gap analysis to ensure focus remains on the most critical goals.

CBM USE CASE 2: Strategic Profiles for Capabilities

Objective: Determine which capabilities should be standardized, differentiated, or innovative based on strategic goals.

Process:
1 Assess each capability to decide if it should adhere to market standards, be organized for cost efficiency or differentiated service, or a focus for innovation.

Outcome:
- Clear strategic decisions and guidance on how each capability should be managed and developed.

- Visual indicators on the Capability Map to denote the strategic orientation of each capability.

CBM USE CASE 3: SWOT Analysis for Capabilities

Objective: Identify strengths, weaknesses, opportunities, and threats (SWOT) for each capability to inform strategic planning.

Process:

1   Conduct a SWOT analysis for each capability to evaluate its current state and future potential.

2   Use the insights to develop strategies that leverage strengths, address weaknesses, exploit opportunities, and mitigate threats.

Outcome:

- A comprehensive understanding of each (assumed) capability's strategic position.

- Informed decision-making for capability development and resource allocation.

CBM USE CASE 4: Operational Resource Mapping

Objective: Align organizational resources with capabilities to ensure effective and efficient use of resources.

Process:

1   Map resources such as personnel, technology, etc. to the capabilities they support.

2   Identify gaps and overlaps in resource allocation to optimize resource distribution.

Outcome:

- Enhanced visibility of resource utilization.

- Improved alignment of resources with strategic priorities.

CBM USE CASE 5: Fit-Gap Analysis

Objective: Identify gaps between current capabilities and those required to achieve strategic goals.

Process:

1   Conduct a detailed analysis to compare existing capabilities with the desired future state.

2   Identify gaps that need to be addressed through development, acquisition, or reorganization.

Outcome:

- A first clear base for a roadmap for capability development.

- Strategic initiatives prioritized based on identified gaps and linked to previously defined strategic importance.

CBM USE CASE 6: Outsourcing

Objective: Determine which capabilities can be outsourced to enhance efficiency and focus on core competencies.

Process:

1   Evaluate each capability to assess its suitability for outsourcing.

2   Identify potential outsourcing partners and develop outsourcing strategies.

Outcome:

- Strategic decisions on which capabilities to outsource.

- Improved focus on core capabilities and better fit with the envisioned strategic profile.

CBM USE CASE 7: Capability Integration and Standardization Profiles (CISPs)

Objective: Make decisions on the levels of integration and standardization of capabilities across the organization to ensure consistency and efficiency where desired and allow for innovation and differentiation where needed. Find synergies and optimize.

Process:

1   Develop profiles for each capability to guide integration and standardization efforts.

2   Implement processes and systems according to these profiles to support the execution of the strategic vision and find synergies.

Outcome:

* Clear guidelines for capability deployment across multiple subsidiaries.

* For example, consistent execution of capabilities across the organization where desired.

* For example, enhanced efficiency and reduced variability in capability performance where desired.

CBM USE CASE 8: Accountability and Responsibility Assignment

Objective: Assign clear accountability and responsibility for each capability to ensure effective management and execution.

Process:

1   Define roles and responsibilities for each capability.

2   Assign ownership and accountability to individuals or teams.

Outcome:

* Clear lines of accountability and responsibility for each capability.

* Improved management and execution of capabilities.

NOTES

[1] Nathan Bennett and G. James Lemoine. "What a difference a word makes: Understanding threats to performance in a VUCA world". In: *Business Horizons* 57.3 (May 2014), pp. 311–317. ISSN: 00076813. DOI: 10.1016/j. bushor.2014.01.001. URL: https:// linkinghub.elsevier.com/ retrieve/pii/S0007681314000020.

[2] Niels Vandevenne, Jonas Van Riel, and Geert Poels. "Green Enterprise Architecture (GREAN)—Leveraging EA for environmentally sustainable digital transformation". In: *Sustainability (Switzerland)* 15.19 (2023). ISSN: 20711050. DOI: 10.3390/ su151914342.

[3] S. Viaene. *Digital Transformation Know How: Connecting Digital Transformation, Agility and Leadership*. Leuven: ACCO, 2020. ISBN: 9789463798136.

[4] Rutendo Mushore and Michael Kyobe. "Optimizing the business value of digital transformation by aligning technology with strategy, work practices and stakeholder interests". In: *2019 IEEE 10th Annual Information Technology, Electronics and Mobile Communication Conference, IEMCON 2019*. 2019. DOI: 10.1109/IEMCON.2019.8936263.

[5] Jeanne W. Ross et al. "Designing and executing digital strategies". In: *2016 International Conference on Information Systems, ICIS 2016* (2016), pp. 1–17.

[6] Frank Grave, Rogier Van De Wetering, and Rob Kusters. "Enterprise Architecture artifacts facilitating digital transformations' strategic planning process". In: *14th IADIS International*

Conference Information Systems. IADIS Press, Mar. 2021. ISBN: 9789898704276. DOI: 10.33965/is2021{_}202103L006. URL: http://www.iadisportal. org/digital-library/enterprise-architecture-artifactsfacilitating-digital-transformations-strategic-planningprocess.

[7] Frank Grave, Rogier Van de Wetering, and Rob Kusters. "How EA information drives digital transformation: A multiple case study and framework". In: *2022 IEEE 24th Conference on Business Informatics (CBI)*. Vol. 1. IEEE, June 2022, pp. 176–185. ISBN: 978-1-6654-6016-3. DOI: 10.1109/CBI54897. 2022.00026. URL: https://ieeexplore.ieee.org/document/9944756/.

[8] Jonas Van Riel and Geert Poels. "A method for developing generic Capability Maps". In: *Business & Information Systems Engineering* 65.2 (Mar.2023). ISSN: 2363-7005. DOI: 10.1007/ s12599-023-00793-z. URL: https://link.springer.com/10.1007/ s12599-023-00793-z.

[9] Michael J. Lenox Jared D. Harris. *The Strategist's Toolkit.* Darden Business Publishing, 2013, p. 131. ISBN: 1615981977, 9781615981977.

[10] G. Hamel and C.K. Prahalad. *"Competing for the Future.* Harvard Business Press, 1996. ISSN: 0033-6807. DOI: 10.1111/j.1467-9310.1996. tb00945.x.

[11] Steven Alter and Narasimha Bolloju. "A Work System front end for object-oriented analysis and design". In: *International Journal of Information Technologies and Systems Approach* 9. January-June (2016), pp. 1–18.

[12] Edith Penrose. *The Theory of the Growth of the Firm.* Oxford University Press, 1959.

[13] Birger Wernerfelt. "A resource-based view of the firm". In: *Strategic Management Journal* 5.2 (Apr. 1984), pp. 171–180. ISSN: 0143-2095. DOI: 10.1002/ smj.4250050207.

[14] Jay Barney. "Firm resources and sustained competitive advantage". In: *Journal of Management* 17.1 (1991), pp. 99–120. ISSN: 15571211. DOI: 10.1177/014920639101700108.

[15] David J. Teece. "The evolution of the Dynamic Capabilities Framework". In: *FGF Studies in Small Business and Entrepreneurship.* 2023. DOI: 10.1007/978-3-031-11371-0{_}6.

[16] David J Teece, Gary Pisano, and Amy Shuen. "Dynamic capabilities and strategic management". In: *Strategic Management Journal* 18.7 (1997), pp. 509–533.

[17]   Matthias Wißotzki. "The Capability Management Process: Finding your way into capability engineering". In: *Business Architecture Management*. Springer, 2015, pp. 77–105. DOI: 10.1007/978-3-319-14571-6{_}5. URL: http://link.springer.com/10.1007/978-3-319-145716_5.

[18]   Jelena Zdravkovic, Janis Stirna, and Janis Grabis. "A Comparative Analysis of Using the Capability Notion for comparative analysis of using the capability notion for congruent business and information systems engineering". In: *Complex Systems Informatics and Modeling Quarterly* 10 (2017), pp. 1–20. ISSN: 2255-9922. DOI: 10.7250/csimq.2017-10.01.

[19]   R. S. Kaplan and D. P. Norton. "Strategy maps: Converting intangible assets into tangible outcomes". *Harvard Business Press*, 2004. ISBN: 978-1-59139-134-0.

[20]   R. S. Kaplan and D. P. Norton. *The Execution Premium: Linking Strategy to Operations for Competitive Advantage*. Harvard Business Press, 2008. ISBN: 9781-4221-2116-0.

[21]   M. Beer and N. Nohria. "Cracking the code of change". In: *Harvard Business Review* 78.3 (2000). ISSN: 00178012. DOI: 10.1007/978-1-137-16511-4{_}4.

[22]   The Open Group. *ACMM Scoring Characteristics for Each Level of the Maturity Model*. Apr. 2022.

[23]   Object Management Group (OMG). *Business motivation model specification (BMM)* v.1.3. 2015. URL: https://www.omg.org/spec/BMM/1.3/.

[24]   Marco Vicente, Nelson Gama, and Miguel Mira Da Silva. "A business motivation model for it service management". In: *International Journal of Information System Modeling and Design* 5.1 (2014). ISSN: 19478194. DOI: 10. 4018/ijismd.2014010104.

[25]   Marilyn M. Helms and Judy Nixon. "Exploring SWOT analysis—where are we now? A review of academic research from the last decade". In: *Journal of Strategy and Management* 3.3 (2010). ISSN: 17554268. DOI: 10.1108/17554251011064837.

[26]   James W Grenning. "Planning poker, or how to avoid analysis paralysis while release planning". In: *Hawthorn Woods Renaissance Software Consulting* 3 (2002).

[27]   Len Bass, Paul Clements, and Rick Kazman. *Software Architecture in Practice Second Edition, Third Edition*. 2013.

[28]   Johnny Saldaña. "Coding and analysis strategies". In: *The Oxford Handbook of Qualitative Research*. 2014. DOI: 10.1093/oxfordhb/9780199811755.013.001.

[29] University of Missouri System. *Business Continuity Management.* Feb. 2024.

[30] Elena Doval. "Is outsourcing a strategic tool to enhance the competitive advantage?" In: *Review of General Management* 23.1 (2016).

[31] Jakki J. Mohr, Sanjit Sengupta, and Stanley F. Slater. "Mapping the outsourcing landscape". In: *Journal of Business Strategy* 32.1 (2011). ISSN: 02756668. DOI: 10.1108/02756661111100319.

[32] Jeanne W. Ross, Peter Weill, and David Robertson. *Enterprise Architecture as Strategy: Creating a Foundation for Business Execution.* Harvard Business Press, 2006, pp. 25–44. ISBN: 1-59139-839-8.

[33] ISACA. Cobit 5: *Enabling Processes.* 2012. ISBN: 978-1-60420-250-2.

[34] Gregory Vial. *Understanding digital transformation: A review and a research agenda.* 2019. DOI: 10.1016/j.jsis.2019.01.003.

[35] M Lynne Markus et al. "The digital transformation conundrum: Labels, definitions, phenomena, and theories". 24.2 (2023), pp. 328–335. DOI: 10.17705/1jais.00809.

[36] Peter C. Verhoef et al. "Digital transformation: A multidisciplinary reflection and research agenda". In: *Journal of Business Research* 122 (2021). ISSN: 01482963. DOI: 10.1016/j.jbusres.2019.09.022.

[37] Jonas Van Riel, Geert Poels, and Stijn Viaene. "Exploring capability mapping as a tool for digital transformation: Insights from a case study". In: *Lecture Notes in Business Information Processing.* Vol. 479 LNBIP. 2023. DOI: 10.1007/978-3-031-34241-7{_}17.

[38] Robert Goodland. "The concept of environmental sustainability". In: *Sustainability.* 2017. DOI: 10.4324/9781315241951-20.

[39] Huwei Wen, Chien Chiang Lee, and Ziyu Song. "Digitalization and environment: How does ICT affect enterprise environmental performance?" In: *Environmental Science and Pollution Research* 28.39 (2021). ISSN: 16147499. DOI: 10.1007/s11356-021-14474-5.

[40] Andreas Freitag. *Applying Business Capabilities in a Corporate Buyer M&A Process.* 2015. DOI: 10.1007/978-3-658-07282-7.

[41] Tyron Offerman, Christoph Johann Stettina, and Aske Plaat. "Business capabilities: A systematic literature review and a

research agenda". In: *2017 International Conference on Engineering, Technology and Innovation (ICE/ITMC)*. 2017, pp. 383–393.

[42] Georgios Koutsopoulos. "A synthesis of diverse organizational capability typologies and classifications". In: *CEUR Workshop Proceedings*. Vol. 3645. 2023.

[43] Porter, M. E. *The Competitive Advantage: Creating and Sustaining Superior Performance*. NY: Free Press, 1985. (Republished with a new introduction, 1998.)

[44] Porter, M. E. *Competitive Strategy: Techniques for Analyzing Industries and Competitors*. New York: Free Press, 1980. (Republished with a new introduction, 1998.)

[45] Gartner. *Accelerating Innovation by Adopting a Pace-Layered Application Strategy*. Jan. 2012. URL: https://www.gartner.com/en/documents/1890915.

[46] SAP LeanIX. (2024). *Expert guide—Using the Gartner® TIME framework for application rationalization* [E-book]. Retrieved February 13, 2025, from https://www.leanix.net/en/download/applying-the-gartner-time-framework-for-application-rationalization